TURNING YOUR
INSIDE OUT

Maxine Burns

AuthorHouse™
1663 Liberty Drive
Bloomington, IN 47403
www.authorhouse.com
Phone: 833-262-8899

Because of the dynamic nature of the Internet, any web addresses or links contained in this book may have changed since publication and may no longer be valid. The views expressed in this work are solely those of the author and do not necessarily reflect the views of the publisher, and the publisher hereby disclaims any responsibility for them.

Any people depicted in stock imagery provided by Getty Images are models, and such images are being used for illustrative purposes only.
Certain stock imagery © Getty Images.

Scripture quotations marked KJV are from the Holy Bible, King James Version (Authorized Version). First published in 1611. Quoted from the KJV Classic Reference Bible, Copyright © 1983 by The Zondervan Corporation.

New International Version (NIV)
Holy Bible, New International Version®, NIV® Copyright ©1973, 1978, 1984, 2011 by Biblica, Inc.® Used by permission. All rights reserved worldwide.

New Living Translation (NLT)
Holy Bible, New Living Translation, copyright © 1996, 2004, 2015 by Tyndale House Foundation. Used by permission of Tyndale House Publishers, Inc., Carol Stream, Illinois 60188. All rights reserved.

This book is printed on acid-free paper.

ISBN: 978-1-6655-6723-7 (sc)
ISBN: 978-1-6655-6722-0 (e)

Library of Congress Control Number: 2022914150

Print information available on the last page.

Published by AuthorHouse 08/08/2022

authorHOUSE®

DEDICATION

This book is dedicated to all the wonderful people that I grew up with in Millwood, Virginia. Growing up in Millwood during the 1950s through the 1970s was a learning experience that sometimes had its ups and downs, primarily because we sometimes did not understand why we had to do chores, or why we were taught responsibilities. We didn't know at the time that our parents were preparing us for adulthood, by teaching us required life skills that would prove beneficial to us throughout our lives.

During those times, everyone's parent served as everyone's parent, and we respected those parents because they always provided wisdom to us. We probably didn't value or appreciate those people until we grew up and moved on. We were taught responsibility and respect for ourselves and others and that honesty was an asset. We always attended Sunday school and went to church on Sundays.

As kids we were taught to pray to God for help in time of need. Back then, I don't think we understood the true magnitude of God's love for us all. I thought that when we prayed for something, we would get it automatically as a result of our prayers. Little did I know that patience and time had to catch up with my faith in God for me to truly understand how prayer and faith work hand in hand and God's timing is always right.

The world and events have changed tremendously since the 1950s, but I still believe that the 3 Rs (Respect, Responsibility, and Regard for others) are still relevant in rearing children of today.

Join me on this journey to visit the years of 1950s to the 1970s in the town of Millwood, Virginia, and meet the people I grew up with. They were all loving and kind people who dearly cared about the children (then) who grew up there during that time. Welcome to Millwood, Virginia, in the 1950s through the1970s.

INTRODUCTION

My name is Maxine Burns, and I grew up in a small village in Virginia (Clarke County) called Millwood. In the mid-1950s, Millwood was my world and my haven. All of our neighbors were like family. They all took on the roles of mother, father, brother, sister, and teachers. They were all loving, kind, and supportive of all the children raised here. We were all taught to respect ourselves and others, to be honest, and to work hard for everything we received. We all attended church and Sunday school every Sunday. We all had chores to do around our homes, and we completed them before going out to play.

Two events that happened when I was younger could have changed the course of my life, had it not been for the grace of God. Number 1 was that my dad died of a heart attack when I was about five years old. Even though I was young, I still remember the games he used to play with my brother and me. I truly loved this man with all my heart and missed him so very much. This had a profound effect on me as I grew up without my father. I missed the hugs and kisses from him, and I've been unable to relate to Father's Day or any day related to fathers, even to this very day. Even though I still had my mother, a father is special to a young girl. My mother reared my sisters and my brother very well, but there was still something missing in my life, and that was a father figure.

Number 2 was that as a kid, I suffered from stuttering or stammering, and I was unable to get my words out without stumbling over them. It often took me up to five minutes to get a word out, and a lot of times the kids in my class would laugh at me. I was often hurt and embarrassed. As I look back now, I could not blame them because we were all just in first grade, and they didn't know any better. My teachers were always supportive of me and tried to the best of their abilities to help me. They talked to the principal on behalf of all the children who had speech problems. My principal, Mr. Ratcliffe, went all out to ask for funding for a speech therapist to help all of us. God bless his heart, that same year funding was approved.

I got the help that I needed, and my symptoms improved as time went on. The underlying cause was still to be determined because even though my speech improved, my self-esteem and my ability to clearly communicate with others had been damaged severely. I was able to mask the underlying cause for a while, but it's funny that when the root cause of anything is not identified, it always resurfaces in one form or another.

I believe that God knew my dilemma, so as my life went on and I graduated and left Millwood, He continued to put great people in my life to help me. I began to believe that God knew me better than I knew myself. He is my therapist, my doctor, my lawyer, my everything, but most of all, He is my friend. All these professions of people were supplied to me at no cost; they all came in the form of a friend. It seemed as if God had handpicked these people because He knew just what I needed to survive.

We all have great intentions to thank people who have been good to us, but like me, we let too much time go by, hours turn into days, days to months and months to years. I let a lot of time go by, suffering from the illness of procrastination. Someone once told me a quote: "Procrastination is the thief of time." Now I know that for every hour I dawdle, something like two months slips away from me, and over the course of time, that space will be obliterated and cease to exist. Time will swallow up those months, and they will be lost forever. If you've got something to do, do it today. "Tomorrow is not promised to anyone."

Most of the people of Millwood that I have spoken of have passed on, but I want their memory to last, never to be forgotten. History is a significant part of who we are now and who we intend to be in the future. These people that I will identify as you read were the cornerstone of our little village. Through this book, I just want to say, "Thank you a thousand times for being in my life, and I love every one of you with all my heart."

You will enjoy reading my book as you take the journey of life with me, while meeting the people who helped rear all the children in my neighborhood, Millwood, Virginia.

CONTENTS

CHAPTER 1

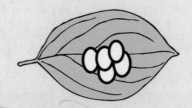

MY FOUNDATION, MY ROCK: MILLWOOD, VIRGINIA

I grew up in a little town called Millwood, Virginia. Millwood is an unincorporated community located in Clarke County, some seventy-five miles from Washington, DC, and is the home of many of Clarke County's most historic sites including the Burwell-Morgan Mill, Carter Hall, the Greenway Historic District, Long Branch, Old Chapel, and the River House. Project HOPE is based at Carter Hall.

I am so proud of this beautiful town, but I remember it most from when I grew up here in the 1950s and 60s. Millwood has changed a lot, and most of the people who once lived here have now passed on. I wrote this book so that the memory of these people, who were the foundation of our community when I was a kid, will live on in the hearts of their children, grands, and great grands. They all deserve this recognition because of the love that came from their hearts, and that love was extended to us.

I realize that time does not stand still and that progress continues everywhere. My story needs to be told because of the uniqueness of the people who lived here. They had very little money or free time, as they worked as long as ten to twelve hours per day providing for their families. These men and women literally made something out of nothing. They made every minute of every day count for something positive, and they always saw that the children of Millwood were taken care of How I loved every last one of these people.

As you began reading this story, please note that just about everyone in Millwood had a nickname. Most references to ladies who had the first name Mary, we shortened it by calling them Ms. Mer. Even today, at seventy years of age, I still know the people I grew up with only by their nicknames.

I laugh as I remember some of the antics that my brother and I got into when we were younger. I remember my brother Bubby running the entire distance of our yard trying to catch the school bus as it was pulling off. He was only about four years old, but he didn't understand why this bus was taking away his two older sisters to school. He then would cry because he didn't understand, and I would give him a hug. I was only five, but we ran and played together until my sisters came home from school. I remember this event just like it was yesterday. Funny how some things are etched in your mind for a lifetime.

Along with other mothers in Millwood, my mother, Mrs. Agnes Burns, went to work early every morning, somewhere around seven o'clock, and didn't return home until about eight p.m.

We didn't have a furnace to just cut on; we had a wood and coal stove, and my mother got up early each morning to make a fire. Bless her heart, she had to use wood, coal, and kerosene to start the stove. We had linoleum on our kitchen floor, and in the early morning that floor was bitterly cold. My mother use to buy wood and coal from a man in White Post, Virginia. I still remember him parking the truck in our yard and unloading the wood and coal into our smokehouse.

I can still hear my mother calling to wake us up in the morning. Her voice would be very calm in the beginning. She would say, "Y'all wake up," and if we didn't move, her tone got louder. Finally she would say, "Y'all get up out of that bed right now!" That was the tone that hit the spot, and we would jump out of bed and get our clothes on. We didn't have bathrooms, but we had basins and a big silver tub that we bathed in.

My mother, along with other mothers worked very hard in people's homes, washing windows, scrubbing floors, making beds, and cooking three meals a day for these households. Back then, I don't think my mother and the other women who worked for these people were treated very well. When my mother went to work, my brother and I stayed with my cousin Ruth during the day. She and her husband, Cousin Winfield, lived up the road from us. Cousin Ruth was a strong black woman who everyone loved and respected. When I got older, I thought of her as a Harriet Tubman type of woman. She was always fighting for the rights of others.

One night there was an incident of some strange men riding through Millwood, trying to bring harm to our community. My mother immediately took me; my brother, Bubby; and my sisters, Lois and Patricia up to Cousin Ruth' s house for shelter, and Cousin Ruth stood up at her window all night long to make sure that no one harmed us. The next morning, the men had gone. I'm not sure if they stopped at her house that night because we went to sleep, but when we woke up, she was still standing there. From that point on, she became my hero.

Once when I was younger, Cousin Ruth was babysitting us in the wintertime, and it was really cold outside and snowing. While she was busy washing clothes, Bubby and I decided that we were going to go sleigh riding in her backyard. We didn't have sleds, so we got innovative and slid down the hill on our bare stomachs. We were having fun and didn't realize that we could have caught pneumonia. Needless, to say, when Cousin Ruth saw us, we both thought we were in trouble. Cousin Ruth saw us out the side window and came to our rescue. She dried us off, put warm clothes on us, sat us in front of the stove, and gave us some hot tea—and told us not to do that anymore.

Funny, how things happen so many years ago and we can recall them just like they happened today. My long memory has always been better than my short memory. I guess it was because we were surrounded by so much love growing up in this small town.

Cousin Ruth would wash her clothes in the tub, using a scrub board, and then wring the clothes out sometimes by hand. She used a soap called Fels-Naptha, still being sold at the Giant, I believe. I just found this product in my grocery store, to my surprise. When she hung those clothes out on the line to dry, they were quite pretty and white. The outside air made them smell good as they dried. She would then bring them in and get them prepared to be ironed. She would have a bowl with water in it on the table. She would then roll the piece of clothing in a ball, and take her hands and sprinkle water mixed with starch over each piece of clothing; then she would iron them. After she ironed the clothes, the starch made them look like they were professionally done—and they were done professionally by Ruth. After she finished ironing, she would then fold each piece of clothing and put them in a big laundry basket for the people she worked for to come and pick up.

Cousin Ruth was definitely a one-of-a-kind strong, phenomenal lady. I would go to visit her almost every Saturday morning after I completed my housework. I still remember what her house looked like. You would walk up the steps through the gate and prayed that Spooky, her dog, was locked up; I was not sure if he would bite, but he definitely barked loudly. Everyone in Millwood was afraid of him. When you entered her house, there was a short hallway that led to the living room, a small pantry, and then the kitchen. They had a back porch that you had to be careful of walking on, because of loose floorboards. As I recall, the upstairs had two bedrooms, one on each side of the hallway.

I would come in and sit in the living room while Cousin Ruth worked in the house. She would be ironing with an iron that you heated up on the stove. I can still see her pick up the iron from the stove, spit on her finger, and touch the iron to see if it was the right temperature. She ironed shirts for a rich family in Millwood. She ironed to perfection; after she got finished those shirts looked like they came from a professional institution. While she worked, I would read her *Abundant Life* magazines. I just enjoyed being in her company.

I still remember this wonderful lady, Cousin Ruth, walking down the road to do her shopping—her dealings as was called back then. She was a strong lady who wore black shoes with a small heel. She always carried her grocery bag in her arms. She would be heading to Locke's store, which was about four blocks away. Phil and Opie, who were the proprietors of that store at the time, were very nice to the people of Millwood. They established credit for just about everyone in town, to ensure that if someone needed something, they could readily get it. These two men were an integral part of our community.

It would take her about three hours to go and come back from the store. You might ask, why three hours? It was because she stopped to talk to everyone on the road, sitting down on everyone's porch to inquire about their family. She would start at the beginning of town and talk with Mrs. Madeline Johnson and her children, Ann, Betty, Jennifer, Inez, Pum, and Bennie. Next door to them was Mrs. Mary Susan Herbert and her family. Also living on the road was Mr. Richard Potter. He used to cater a lot of parties, always dressed clean as a whistle. I think he drove a light greenish Studebaker.

She would then holler across the road to Mr. and Mrs. Bismarck Walker and their children, Mutt, Jeff, and Anna. Anna was a go-getter: a cheerleader, she also took part in many school sports such as basketball. She was a great player. I believe Mutt and Jeff as excellent baseball, basketball, and football players. Millwood was loaded with talented youngsters.

She would then talk to Mrs. Edith Harris, her mother, and Cousins Jenny, Jeanette, and Barbara. Cousin Jenny had the most beautiful white hair. Edith, Jeanette, and Barbara were also very loving and kind people who loved everyone in the neighborhood. I also remember Mrs. Luvenia Mason, who lived on the curve coming into Millwood from Boyce. She was a small-built lady who use to walk to Locke's store with a shopping cart to get her groceries. Such a nice, kind, and loving person.

Further down the road, she would stop to see Ms. Mary Randolph, Ms. Massie, Mr. Charlie Williams, and his wife, Mrs. Beatrice. I remember Mr. Charlie and Ms. Bee sitting out on their back porch. They were such a loving couple. Cousin Ruth would then come and sit on our front porch and talk to my mother, Mrs. Agnes Burns. She was now at the halfway point on her trip to the store. Mind you, everyone on the road deserved at least thirty minutes of her time, and all of her talk was good and positive, as she was concerned and loved all of her neighbors.

Next door to us was Mrs. Mary Dorsey (known as Ms. Mer). Residing with Ms. Mer were her daughter Georgie and her granddaughter Cheryl. Jessie was her son who also lived in the house. One time Jessie got a puppy that he named King. I have always loved animals, and I kind of adopted King. He was a German shepherd dog. As he grew, he became my friend, and every morning I would get up and yell, "King! Here, King," and he would come running from wherever he was at that time, and we would play. Ms. Mer kept him in his doghouse in her back yard. He was such a great dog, rather large with a tannish brown coat. He was my friend growing up.

Cousin Ruth would then go down the road visiting each one of our neighbors. The first were Buddy Boy and Ruth, who had two children, a daughter named Gilda Marie and a son, Claude. They were the most loving people that I have ever seen on this earth. Then came Ms. Nannie Randolph, her daughter we called Bug (her nickname), Thomas (Bug's husband), and their children, Barbara Ann, Jeanette, Gwenny, Jitter, and Bunny. I can still see Ms. Nannie crossing the road with a cup of coffee in her hands going to Big Sister's house across the road for their early morning chat.

Cousin Ruth also made stops at Sister Randolph's, where she and her husband Marshall lived. I believe Marshall worked in Winchester hospital, and he would catch the Greyhound bus home every evening. I can still see Sister Randolph hanging on that fence talking to people going up and coming down the road. She was such a happy lady, always had a smile on her face.

She would then stop by to visit Mrs. Catherine Jackson; her husband, Mr. Francis; and their children, Miranda, Cathy, Mickey, Barron, and John Francis. Ms. Catherine also baked a fantastic applesauce cake, and she would always share with us. Of course, Cousin Ruth, always remembered to stop and see Mr. Holmes; he always had funny stories to tell us, plus words of wisdom; such a phenomenal man. Mr. Holmes was a member of our little village and was also our seventh-grade teacher. He lived next door to Shiloh Church. He was a true genius, such a smart man who could conjugate a verb like no one else

She also visited the people living on Millwood Hill. I still remember Mrs. Sophie Sanford and her husband, who we called Mr. Sanford. Mrs. Sophie was a hardworking woman who put together a lot of activities for the kids in Millwood. She had the spirit of Sojourner Truth. When she spoke, people listened. Her children were Jonathan, Little Robby, Roddy, and Wesley. Her sister, Mrs. Mary Mason, lived on the hill also; she was a good friend of my mother's. She and my mother would walk to visit each other during the weekends. Mrs. Mer was married to Mr. Eddie, and their children were Susan, Sis, Poose, Bobby, Ann, Baby Sister, and Betty Lou. I also remember Mrs. Mamie Jackson and her niece we called Knee-Knee which was short for Ms. Denise Jackson. Ms. Denise had brothers named Kevin and Douglas.

Also along that road lived Mrs. Doris Green and her children, Toni, Chris, Sharon, and Pauline. Doris's siblings were Ms. Rosetta and her husband, Marvin (we called him chummy), and their children, Rolanda, Mark, and Kendall. Ms. Rosetta also had sisters and brothers named, George, Patricia, and Eugene (Gene). Ms. Rosetta was a very fashionable lady who always looked beautiful in her clothes. She along with so many other women helped to organize a lot of activities for the kids in our community. She also chaperoned a lot of dances that we attended at the recreation center. All were such fantastic people always willing to help their community. Gene, Ronnie, Jeff, Mutt and my brother Bubby were just some of the young men who excelled in sports, they were our sports heroes. Also on the hill were Mrs. Elizabeth (Pucat) Banks and her husband, Junior. Their children were Michael, David Wayne, and Kelly.

A couple of doors away, going up the hill, lived Mr. Spair Pendleton and his wife Mrs. Gladys. They had three children: Elaine, Douglas, and Kevin.

I also like to include Browntown as a part of Millwood. I remember Mrs. Elsie Cook and her husband John along with their children, Leslie, John, and Mary. Further up were Futes and his wife Cornelia, and their children, Jennifer, Debbie, Adam, and Timothy. Rev. Alan Williams and his family lived there along with their children, Daisy Jane, Ollie, and Margaret. These were dedicated church people who truly loved God with all their hearts, and they attended Guildfield Baptist Church every Sunday.

I dearly remember Rev. and Mrs. Charlie Roberts. They were such a loving couple. Wherever you saw one, you saw the other. They lived next to Locke's store. Her daughter and son-in-law, Mr. and Mrs. William Marshall, would frequently come to visit them. They would also bring their children, Clarence, Debbie, Vickie, and Tunsall. We all would play and have fun.

Mr. and Mrs. Francis Pendleton were always there to help anybody in need, whether you needed a ride to the store or just someone to talk to. He had a fashionable kind of walk. He was married to Mrs. Mer Pendleton, who was a sweet, loving, and kind mother, grandmother, and friend. They also had three children, Ronnie, Rita, and Stephanie, three loving, kind people. Mr. Francis was sometimes known as the mayor of Millwood because he always was there to help people.

Also on the road were Mr. and Mrs. William Brown Layton. Mr. Layton was a tall man with gray hair who supported his community by taking his neighbors to and from the grocery store and to the doctor or to the hospital; wherever the need was, he was always present. Mrs. Layton was a short lady, very pretty, and nice to everyone. They lived in the big house across from the mill.

Mrs. Rosy Pendleton's children I only knew by their nicknames: Spair, Skinny, Anna Mae, Pearline, and Mollie. Then there were her grandchildren, Altire, Cynthia, Jackie, Brenda, Bruce, Ricky, JoJo, and Junior Baby. They were a tight-knit and loving family who always looked out for each other and were very kind and loving to their neighbors.

Ms. RoseAnn Williams and her family also lived on the road. Everyone in Millwood loved RoseAnn, as she was hardworking and loving to everyone. She would give anyone the shirt off her back. She was one of my favorite people in Millwood. One Christmas I wanted to give her a present, but I didn't have any money. I thought and thought about what I could give her. Finally, knowing that she liked potatoes, I asked my mother if I could give her a gift of two potatoes, and my mother said yes. I wrapped them up in Christmas wrap and gave them to her. I thought she was going to laugh, but she gave me a big hug and said thank you. That was the kind of person she was, a very loving and appreciative person.

I remember RoseAnn's mother; I believe we called her "Little Sister," and her husband we called Bobby. They were such loving and kind people. RoseAnn also had a son named Brian and raised her nieces and nephews, Valerie, Karen, Janice, Robbie, and *********.

Next to them on the road were Mr. and Mrs. Logan Jones. Mrs. Georgiana Jones was the lady who taught me how to drive. After I got my learner's permit, she allowed me to drive her car to Berryville (she went with me), and we came around the corner a little too fast, but I stopped in time to make my turn. She was very patient and never fussed at me. She told me to keep driving and not to give up, and I did keep driving. She had one daughter named Audrey, who was the love of her life. I believe she shared her house with her mother and grandmother; they were a very close and loving family. We got our first dog, Pudgy, from Georgiana. Georgianna and her family loved animals and people.

I also remember Mr. and Mrs. Bennie Carter. He was a short, thin man who drove a big station wagon, maybe a Chevrolet, and his wife, Ms. Henrietta, taught us at Sunday school. They both were very kind and loving people in Millwood.

I also remember the small church up on the hill, next to the cemetery. Rev. Roy Pollard would preach at that church during the weekends, and I made sure that I attended the services. His sons, Archie, Stevie, and Percy, would be playing the guitars, and their sister Jessie would be singing and praising God. How I loved being in their presence. They sang and played so many beautiful songs, sung from the heart, and Rev. Pollard was a great speaker.

I also remember Mrs. Mary Randolph; her son, Mr. Joe Randolph; and her daughter Mrs. Beadie Randolph Townley. They lived next door to the cemetery. They did a lot of good things in the community, especially Ms. Beadie, as she was our Sunday school teacher and also a great friend.

Some of the people who lived past Locke's store, Cousin Ruth was unable to visit because the distance was so far, but she always inquired around town about those she didn't get to see too often.

Mrs. Louise Bannister and Mrs. Hattie Cook were also two ladies who lived in Millwood. I believe Mrs. Louise Bannister was a substitute schoolteacher, and Mrs. Hattie Cook was her best friend. They were two beautiful ladies with their origins in Millwood. Both of these ladies were loving and beautiful people. They were also very stylish and classy.

I'm also reminded of Mrs. Sadie Bannister and her daughters, Sandra, Gail, and Phyllis, who lived on the edge of Millwood. Ms. Sadie had three sisters, who she affectionately called Lillie, Beadie, and Issie. They were all loving and pleasant sisters and were very close to each other. Sandra was my classmate at school, truly a dear, lovable friend.

I believe living up on the hill from Ms. Sadie's house were Mrs. Edmonia Banks and her family, such fantastic and loving people.

Also living on that road was the Thornton family, Mrs. Beatrice Thornton; her daughters, Betty Lou, Joanne, Pauline, Sue, Juanita, Helen, and Joyce; and her sons, Bennie and Chuck. Mrs. Pauline Thornton was our librarian at Johnson-Williams High School; she knew her librarian duties better than anyone I know, a very smart and studious lady. In the summertime, when we used to go to the recreation center, Chuck, Junior Banks, and the rest of the men in Millwood would get together and play a game of horseshoes. They would play in the back yard adjacent to the creek. While playing horseshoes, Chuck never missed a ringer. He and the other gentlemen of Millwood loved the game of horseshoes. The Thornton family were such a treasure, loved by everyone in the community.

I can also remember Mr. Penn, a short man who sometimes walked with a long stick in his hand. He always was a happy man with a smile on his face. Then there was Ms. Violet Bannister, who lived not far from him, and I believe they both were members of Guildfield Baptist Church. They both were humble church members who every Sunday sang praises and honor to God. I can still see her raking her yard.

Cousin Herman Jackson lived next to Guildfield church. Cousin Herman was Cousin Ruth's brother, and I would walk with her to visit him sometimes. I was so blessed to be in the midst of some of the greatest people on earth. Aw, Millwood, such a great place to grow up; I still have fond memories of this beautiful little village.

Living further down the road were Mr. and Mrs. Raphael Johnson and their daughter, Edna. Raphael was a very pleasant man who greeted everyone with a smile and a handshake. I remember his wife, Bufie, made the best deviled eggs in Millwood. She was a wonderful cook, and everyone truly loved their daughter Edna, who had a great personality and loved everyone. Truly a God-blessed family.

I also had an uncle named Mr. Marshall Mason who lived on the outskirts of Millwood. He and his father shared a home there. Uncle Marshall was a tall man who walked kind of bent over. I believe it was because he had worked so very hard in his lifetime. He was a loving man who would walk to our house once a week and sit down and talk to my mother. It was about eight blocks from his house to our house. We truly loved this man.

I remember every Christmas, Bubby and I would get into bed around seven o'clock before it got dark, because we were so excited about Christmas Day. I still remember sleeping in my bedroom next to the window as I shared a bedroom with my sister Patricia.

At night, I would look out the window across the road to see the light on from the Browns' front porch, and once I saw that light, I felt secure. We almost always had snow for Christmas and as I looked out the window, the snow glistened so beautifully, and my brother and I would then go to sleep while Mama prepared the Christmas tree and put our

12

gifts underneath it. My mother is such a jewel; she would bake ham, turkey, of course fried chicken, potato salad, mashed potatoes, greens, and lots of other food for us. Her specialties were applesauce cake, chocolate cake roll, and coconut cake. I lived for that tasty cake. My mother, bless her heart, would have the house nice and warm for us when we got up. Bubby and I would wake up and immediately go down and look under the Christmas tree and we would each get one piece of clothing and one toy, which was what most of the kids got.

Once everybody woke up, we would sit down to a breakfast fit for a king: waffles, eggs, bacon, and maybe hot chocolate. We didn't have a television set until I was twelve or thirteen, and I remember watching the *Andy Williams Christmas Special*, Bing Crosby, and the *Perry Como Show*. We would then wait until everyone else in the neighborhood was up, and we went visiting. We would also go sleigh riding; now mind you, we didn't have sleds, so we compromised by sliding downhill with large paper boxes. Yes, we were very creative back then.

About noon, we would go visiting. Our first stop would be Ms. Mary Dorsey's house (we affectionately called her Ms. Mer), and she would give us a slice of cake that she had made and something to drink and ask us what we got for Christmas. I can still see the Christmas lights that surrounded her front door; they gleamed against the snow falling outside. So breathtaking. Everyone in our neighborhood had a real tree, decorated with angel hair and tinsel and bulbs (those large beautiful red, green, and blue bulbs). We had ornaments that had been passed down over the years, and we would pray each year that they would continue to work.

When I was a kid, Christmas was a magical time. I believed in Santa Claus until I was about thirteen years old. Such golden years. For some reason, was probably superstition, we always had to take our tree down before New Year's Day.

As I look back today, growing up in this small town was pretty fantastic, with great people working together for the good of the entire community. Work ethics were instilled into everyone at a very early age. Most people in Millwood didn't have indoor plumbing, so we had to go to the well to get water. I remember the silver bucket we used to have to carry the water in. We didn't have any gloves, so water splashed on our hands as we carried the buckets home. I can still feel the cold water splash against my hands.

We also had an outhouse in the back yard and a wood and coal house for storing wood and coal. We got our wood and coal from a man in White Post, Virginia. He would store it in our woodhouse. In the winter when it snowed, most young folks (mainly the boys) would get up early so that they would be the first to shovel someone's walkways to make some money. If an elderly person asked you to go to the store for them, you were not allowed to take money from them, even though that elderly person might want to pay you. We were told that you do kindness for people, and you don't charge them. We also had Sunday school picnics which were organized by women in our community to ensure that we had something to do during the summer months. Aw, those fine beautiful ladies deserve their accolades every day for making our lives so wonderful.

We would go places like Glen Echo and Hershey Park. I remember just like it was yesterday, all of the kids in our community got new clothes to wear on our picnic; wow, such a great time. In Millwood there was not much to do, so to be able to ride on the transport bus taking us out of Millwood was a thrill. I don't want to leave this paragraph without having said that nothing was given to any of us free of charge. We were required to work, and we had to attend church and Sunday school on a regular basis, and we had to respect, love, and help the people in our community. We had to earn all of our privileges mainly because back then our parents did not make a lot of money. All families just barely scraped by, but we all worked together.

The truth be told, we worked all summer long to gain one trip at the end of each summer. As I said, hard work was instilled in us early on. When one family didn't have, the other family gave freely. I can still remember my mother going to our next-door neighbor, Ms. Mer, to borrow a cup of sugar, and she would come to us when she needed the same. The same philosophy floated through our town.

In those days most of our neighbors did not have telephones, and the internet had not even been thought of back then. It still boggles my mind as to how these wonderful ladies carried out all those tasks to bring joy to the children in Millwood. I believe that faith in God and dedication to our community was the driving force that kept these ladies going. You might ask why we all had to work so hard to earn one trip each summer. Hard work and dedication made us the people that we are today. I would like to say that some of this rubbed off. I would be very remiss if I didn't mention those ladies' names that were outstanding in our community.

When I was twelve years old, I wanted to be a majorette. Since my next-door neighbor Cheryl was already one, I thought I would ask her about joining, and she said that she would check it out and let me know. She got back with me after a couple of days and told me to come to tryouts. I went for the tryouts and made the team. I was on cloud nine. On homecoming weekend, we were scheduled to march in a parade, and I just couldn't wait. I was so happy that I would be dressed in my white majorette uniform and wearing my signature majorette boots.

On that Friday we had our last rehearsal because the parade was on Saturday. Our instructor told us that we all looked good and to be at the school at 7:30 on Saturday morning. I was so excited that I barely slept, I could just see myself strutting thru the streets of Berryville, twirling my baton and showing everyone how good we all looked. We all got to the school at 7:30, and about eight it started to rain. My heart began to sink as thoughts of the parade began to fade. We were told that we could still march if we wanted to, but we might get wet. A couple of the majorettes said that they would not march because they had just gotten their hair done, and they were not going to mess it up. I was trying to convince everyone that we should march anyway and that the rain would stop, but the majority ruled, and we did not march.

The parade was supposed to start at noon, and it was still pouring down rain at 12:30. It looked as if it was not going to stop, and it didn't. It poured until about five o'clock. My first shot at stardom, and I was heartbroken because that was the only parade that we had a chance to be in the whole year. I felt that my one and only chance had gone up I smoke. I went back home and was depressed for a while. But in the country you learn how to bounce back, because you learn that there are far more important things (everyday chores, schoolwork, etc.) that require your full attention. I did make a vow to myself that if another chance came up, I was going to be in it. Second chance is now, and I feel it my duty to tell the world about my beautiful life as a kid in Millwood, Virginia.

In May of each year, our parents would take us to the Apple Blossom Parade in Winchester, Virginia. Most of the people from Millwood would catch the Greyhound bus that came through Millwood going to Winchester. We would be so happy because we were also able to go to the carnival—definitely a day of fun. I lived on old Route 50, and that was the route that the Greyhound took to get to Winchester. The highlight of the parade was the Douglas High School marching band, and their drum majorette was Ms. Betty Jo Long, and she put on a very professional show for everyone. We would stand out on the streets of Winchester along with everyone else, watching the parade go by.

In the 1950s and '60s, Millwood was mostly a black community, and most if not all parents had the same rules from one side of town to the other, and every woman in this town was every child's parent. If you did something wrong at school, your parents knew it almost before you did. We always thought that our parents had a radar between their worksite and our school.

There was a weekend ritual for everyone. On Saturday mornings, while our parents went to work, we were all responsible for cleaning our home; this included washing and waxing floors, washing dishes and clothes, hanging clothes up on the line, dusting furniture, and sweeping off the front porch. We could then go out to play, but we had to be back in before our parents got off work, and we were always back home on time. Back then, kids did not defy their parents; it was better to listen than to face the wrath of Khan.

On Saturday nights, we were able to go to the recreation center where George Turner would spin records. We would dance, socialize with our friends, and meet new people, and we could even buy hot dogs and sodas. We listened and danced to music by the Four Tops, "Baby, I Need Your Loving," "Bernadette," and "I Can't Help myself"; the Temptations, "Just My Imagination" and "My Girl"; Otis Redding, "Sitting on the Dock of the Bay"; Al Green, Marvin Gaye, and the Drifters, "This Magic Moment" and "Under the Boardwalk"; and the Cadillac singing "Mr. Earl." I can't forget Jackie Wilson, "Higher and Higher." Aw, seems like it was just yesterday, such an awesome time. Since Millwood had the only recreation center, we attracted many boys and girls from Winchester, Front Royal, and the surrounding counties. Mr. George Turner loved being our DJ; he was so cool.

I think the center closed around ten or eleven each Saturday night. We all had to walk home in the dark; back then there were no streetlights. We all walked home (about two dozen of us), and we had to pass the cemetery going home. As we approached the cemetery, someone would yell out and say something like "I see someone moving in the cemetery," and we all would take off running. I remember my sister Patricia would hold on to my hand and my brother's hand. We kept running until everyone found themselves at their front door, safe at home. Our next-door neighbor, Ms. Mer Dorsey, bless her heart would have her door open and would make sure that we got into the house safely.

This center also served as a recreation center during the summer months; we would have games, lunch, and outdoor activities. We also had swings, seesaws, and sliding boards. There was also a basketball court. We also could buy Nehi sodas from the Soda Machine. I think they cost about twenty-five cents a bottle. My favorite was Nehi grape, I lived for that soda. Since there wasn't much to do in the country, this rec center served as an inspiration for all the young people.

Note: We had to make sure that we had completed all of our housework before we could go to the center. Responsibility was key with all the parents in Millwood. If we wanted to buy sodas, we had to work and earn that twenty-five cents.

On Sunday, our parents would wake up early and listen to the radio, tuned into the Heavenly Gospel Choir from Front Royal, Virginia, which aired from 7:00 to 8:00 a.m. You could hear the gospel music all over this small town because everyone tuned in. As they listened to this great choir, they fried chicken which was our signature meal on Sundays. I remember back then they fried their chicken using lard, which came in a blue box and kind of resembled a big, thick white glob. Since we exercised a lot, it didn't seem to bother us health-wise. After frying the chicken, they would wake us for church. Almost every family had the same routine. For the most part it was an unwritten parent law that we all had to go to church on Sunday, and for the most part we enjoyed going, especially since there was nothing much to do in the country.

Everyone had total respect for Sunday: no dancing, and definitely no listening to rock and roll music. Back then there was something called a blue law that prohibited stores from opening on Sundays. We were told that Sunday was God's day, and it was respected as such by all.

There were two churches in Millwood that mostly were attended by black people. The one closest to where we lived was Shiloh Baptist Church, and that was the one we attended. We had several preachers when I was younger, but I remember specifically Rev. Wilbert Branch as he was very caring to our community. He would visit the seniors and sick and shut-in as well as people in our community who weren't members of this church. He was such a great man of God who loved everyone. He always made everyone feel welcome in our church.

We also had a great choir. I don't recall that we had a piano player, so we sang a cappella. Some of the choir members that I remember were John Henry (our leader), Miranda, Kathy, Cookie, Sylvia, Patricia, Jackie, and Brenda—and of course myself. I am sure there were others, and I give respect and love to all of them. We would attend events such as the Sunday school convention, and we were invited to sing at different churches. John Henry Williams was our choir leader, and he could really sing and led wonderfully. At Easter time we would sing a song called "He Arose"; another song we sang was called "Higher Ground," written by Edward Mote in 1834. The lyrics went a little like this: "Lord, lift me up and let me stand, by faith on heaven's table land. No higher plane that I have found, Lord, plant my feet on higher ground."

I also remember singing "Leaning on the Everlasting Arms," composed by Anthony Johnson Showalter and Elisha Hoffman in 1887. "What a fellowship, what a joy divine, leaning on the everlasting arms."

Our closing hymn each Sunday was always "Blest Be the Tie that Binds," written by John Fawcett in 1772. I can still hear us singing this hymn: "Blest be the tie that binds our hearts in Christian love. The fellowship of kindred minds is like to that above."

The Sunday that we received our choir robes, we were all in heaven, I think we all began to sing better, we felt so professional. One time we were invited to another church to sing, and John Henry and some of the other members of the choir were not able to attend. For some reason I volunteered to lead the choir. I did not have a good singing voice, but I gave it my all. People were very nonjudgmental back then; they just appreciated young people getting up and singing for the Lord. We all got a standing ovation from our audience. Experiences like these you really appreciate, especially when you are young; they encourage you to do more.

19

I also remember two beautiful couples in our community who used to assist our church in transporting the choir members from one location to the next. Mr. and Mrs. Downing Banks and Mr. and Mrs. Bennie Carter were always instrumental in transporting us. Two great families who truly loved their community.

My mind now runs to my Sunday school teachers, Ms. Mary (Mer) Susan Herbert, Mrs. Mary (Mer) Randolph, and her daughter, Ms. Beadie Randolph. At Shiloh Baptist Church in Millwood, Virginia, these ladies served as our Sunday school teachers to children who ranged from eight years old to teenagers. I was about six years old back then. I believe all of the children in Millwood loved these ladies because of their love of God and their dedication and devotion to children. We all loved going to church, but we especially loved going to Sunday school, which started around nine thirty or ten, and church came right after.

They taught us about Jesus and His love for us and how we should always do our best in everything we did, because that is what God wants us to do. We didn't necessarily have to be the best, but we were expected to be *our* best. Those words still carry a lot of weight in my life today.

We also had to learn Bible verses. The twenty-third Psalm was my favorite: "The Lord is my shepherd; I shall not want". At the beginning of our class, we had to recite a Bible verse that we had learned the week before. I was so proud to stand up and say my Bible verse, especially when I took the time to learn the verse. When I didn't rehearse, it was a different story. When Sunday school was over, we were given Bible cards with pictures and Bible verses, so that we would remember them.

We would start practicing for our Christmas program right after Thanksgiving. This program included all of the children in Millwood. These ladies would work with us until we learned all of our lines and were able to present it confidently. When we got up on the stage at church we felt that we could accomplish anything because they instilled that confidence and belief in ourselves. One year I remember my brother (Bubby) and our cousin got up to sing "Silent Night"; they both were very off-key and we all started giggling. Our Sunday school teachers gave us *the look*, and we immediately straightened up. We always were told not to worry about how we sounded; "Just have the nerve to get up on stage and present yourself from beginning to end." They always told us, "It's not important what others think about you, but it is important what you think about yourself." My brother and my cousin presented "Silent Night" to the best of their ability (all the way to the end, two whole verses); afterwards all the parents and community gave them a standing ovation, and they grinned all over themselves because they were so proud.

Another year, I remember another little boy got up to say his Christmas recitation, and he started out well, but all of a sudden he forgot his lines, and he called out to his sister who was sitting in the audience and said, "I thought you said you were going to help me." He was so upset, because his sister embarrassed him by not coming to his rescue. Again as kids we chuckled and again we got *the look* and immediately stopped. Our Sunday school teachers came up to the stage, stood beside him smiling, and helped him through his last three lines. He was proud as a peacock, and before he sat down, he gave them a big hug and said thank you. It bought tears to our eyes. These ladies were so supportive and loving to all of us.

We also had a beautiful tree in church, decorated with beautiful lights, and we each were given an orange, a corsage, and a bag of rock candy along with a candy cane as gifts. The gifts might seem like something small, but they were the most precious gifts that we could ever receive and we greatly appreciated all the efforts that these wonderful ladies put together just for us. We then walked home in the snow thoroughly feeling good inside for all the love we had received. We all had visions of sugar plums dancing in our heads because the next day was Christmas, and all was right with the world.

Guildfield Baptist Church was the church a little further down the road. On the third Sunday of September each year this church would have its union meeting where all churches in that particular union would meet together in Millwood. We lived for the union meeting, as my aunt Lila would come in from Buffalo, and my aunt Hannah would come in from Baltimore. Other relatives of people in our community also descended upon Millwood, and it was happy times all around. Everyone would come and visit and cook food, such a good time of togetherness. We would all go on Sunday to church. I can remember me and my sisters getting ready for church in my mother's house. Makeup had to be in place, stockings, high heels, and of course your best dress or suit.

When I was young, like many of my friends, one of my main goals of attending the union meeting was to meet boys. As we grew and matured, the presence of community, love, respect, and togetherness became more important. The fellowship of the seniors in our community far outweighed anything else. We loved going to church. In Guildfield Church, there were two floors. For the most part, the seniors were downstairs, and the younger folks were upstairs. Before we went upstairs, we were told to be quiet and respect the church, and we did. (Back then we didn't get many spankings, we just got the look. I have never been able to replicate that look.)

We would get into church about 10:45 and church would start promptly at 11:00. I can still can see Rev. Isham Williams sitting up on the pulpit in his chair, rocking back and forth, singing "I'll Fly Away," written by Albert Brumley in 1929.

Some glad morning when this life is over
I'll fly away
To a home on God's celestial shore
I'll fly away
I'll fly away, oh, Glory
I'll fly away
When I die, Hallelujah, by and by
I'll fly away.

22

I believe Rev. Isham, bless his heart, truly loved that song along with everyone else. I even found myself singing along to that beautiful song. He was a true man of God, and he really knew how to bring the word of the Lord to his members and others. I also remember the ushers in their starched white uniforms. The women looked so beautiful. I remember Mr. Francis Pendleton who would have his black suit on and white gloves, one hand behind his back as he ushered people into the church. I also remember the other ushers—Mrs. Gladys Stewart, Mrs. Briscoe, Mrs. Elizabeth Mason, Mrs. Margaret Williams, Mrs. Bessie Robertson, and Mrs. Ollie Williams—and so many others who made that church a heavenly place to visit. They all looked so beautiful in their starched white uniforms. Each time I entered this church, I got swept up in the spirit.

Sometimes, after church, my friends and I helped to serve food to the visiting churches who attended services there. To us, this was exciting because we were helping. Prior to the Sunday meeting, my friends and I volunteered to help cook the food for the visiting churches. We worked all day at the church on Saturday. I remember working with Mrs. Agnes Walker, who was married to Mr. Bis, such a beautiful and loving couple, how I loved this lady, she was so kind and good to everyone. As we cooked food, someone would decide that they would sing a hymn, and that made everything seem all the more special; as we cooked, we heard beautiful music being sung.

We fried chicken and made potato salad, greens, corn pudding, mashed potatoes, and gravy, and of courses the ladies made caramel cake, chocolate cake and coconut cakes. How those beautiful ladies could cook up some food. Of course we also made sweet tea. What a glorious time in the Lord and to be in the presence of these beautiful ladies.

I also remember the baptisms that used to take place in the creek just behind the mill. We all stood on the bank watching as Rev. Isham went into the water. He would have on a long white robe, and he would carry a long stick, almost as tall as he was. As a kid, I assumed the stick was to test the water to ensure that it wasn't too

23

deep. He would then head back to the bank, and there he would pick up his deacon Mr. Francis Pendleton (who was also dressed in a long white robe) and the person(s) who were going to get baptized. They would slowly walk to the point where Rev. Isham left off, while holding onto the arms of the next person to be baptized.

When they arrived at that point, they would stop and pray and sing a hymn. They would then both hold onto the person and take them back in the water, and Rev Isham would say, "I now baptize you in the name of the Father, Son, and the Holy Spirit"; then he would say "Amen." When this person was baptized and brought back up, you could feel the spirit moving over everyone in attendance. Immediately after the baptism the audience would sing "I'll Be All Right Someday." That kind of baptism could only occur back then and was truly meaningful in every way. We would all then walk back to church, sat in the pews and get ourselves ready for church. Truly, truly remarkable. How I miss that kind of true devotion.

I can also remember Mrs. Becky Allen, her daughter Cora, and her brother Otis. What a beautiful and loving family they all were. When you saw one member of the family walking down the road, you saw them all. They were a very close and loving family. Otis was in the same class that I was in; such a great person.

I have very fond memories of Ms. Gladys Stewart and her family: her daughters, Linda Mae and Lena Faye, and their children. They were such a joy to the people in Millwood. They always smiled and treated everyone kindly; they all were very happy people.

We didn't get a television until I was about thirteen, but I remember how excited we were when we found out that a black musical group would be on television. We were excited because it was the first time that black people appeared on television in our area. We went to every house on the road that had a television set and told them what time it would be on. As those singers performed, I would look in their eyes, and they gave their all. I could sense that they felt good about themselves all through their souls. Their music and their voices were pristine. It showed in their faces and their body movements. I thought to myself, *Is that what self-confidence looks like? If so, one day I want to have that same feeling about something that I can do that is good*. This made us all feel good about ourselves and let us know that we all had God-given talents. We just needed to search our souls and bring them to the forefront. I felt that I was a person just like they were, made by the same God, and if they could do it, I could also in one form or another.

At this time the seed was planted. Who would have known I would be seventy years of age before I stepped out and finally exhibited the courage to see my gift(s) through? I can take solace in the fact that I didn't know then what I know now. I believe you can deliver your message at any time in life as long as it's carried out before you leave this earth. When we die, we don't want our "gifts" to die along with us. God gave those gifts specifically to us, and no one can give them life but us. We are the caretakers of what lies within our souls. Release your soul while you are on this earth by giving life to your gifts. There you will be sharing your God-given gift with the world. Bring your gifts to life while you're still here on this earth so that when you are gone, your part in bringing about world peace has been cemented in the puzzle of life. We all have a special contribution that we must make.

I look at our life as one giant puzzle. We all make up that puzzle by having a place where our puzzle piece will fit in. Some puzzle pieces are round, and some are square; that's because we are all different and fit into the puzzle in different ways, but we all fit into our designated spaces. The space that only we can fit in was made specifically for us.

We all are born with special gifts that we must nurture and put into action positively so we can make a change in this world. Some people live short lives, and others live long lives. No matter the length of time we are given on this earth, we all play a significant role in bringing about world peace. We all make up that puzzle of life. We all owe it to God to give life to our special gifts so that the world can benefit. We all owe it to God to do our best, find out what we do best, and bring our gifts to the forefront of our lives. Let your light so shine that the world can see you in the darkness that's trying to overshadow us all.

I now see my mother and the other parents in Millwood with different eyes. They taught us the value of hard work, provided us with a three-course meal every day (and we had to eat everything off our plates). They taught us manners and the value of honesty, and they provided for us royally with Christmas and other holidays. They didn't make much money, but they certainly knew how to stretch a dollar. We were taught to go to church on Sundays and to keep Sunday a holy day. We were taught to help our neighbors when they were in need. What better upbringing could a kid possibly have? Whatever my mother put on our plates, we had to eat it. One time we had asparagus for dinner, and I did not like it. My mother told me I had to sit at the table until I ate it all. I think I got up from the dinner table about eight o'clock that night. That time was significant as it was about five when I started to eat my dinner. I cleaned my plate.

My mother, like all the parents in my hometown, had rules that had to be followed, and we all listened to our parents. Not only did we have love for our parents, but we had respect also. These were the values that shaped our future. Hard work turned us kids into the productive citizens we are today.

In the summertime we used to catch lightning bugs and put them in a jar. We would punch holes in the lid to ensure they got air. We would sit the jar of lightning bugs on our dresser and watch as they lit up the room.

The combination of teachers working together with parents made for a phenomenal team, and I am so grateful that I can claim Millwood, Virginia, and all of the wonderful people that grew up there in the years of 1951 through 1970, my forever hometown.

Millwood Blueprint (as I remember) - 1956 – 1970

As you are coming into Millwood from Boyce, Virginia (passing Powhatan School)

Houses on the right-hand side of the road
(Please note; so sorry if I left off some people, but these are the ones I remember)
Mrs. Mary Susan Herbert and her family – Our Sunday school teacher
Mrs. Madeline Jones and her family
Mr. Hubert Jeffrey
Mrs. Rosetta Mason and her husband Jitter
Mr. Richard Potter.

Houses on the Right
Mr. and Mrs. Bismarck Walker, Jr.
Recreation Center
Mrs. Edith Harris and her family
Cemetery
Ms. Mary Randolph and her family
Mrs. Irene Kent
Ms. Massie
Mr. Charlie Williams and Mrs. Beatrice
Mrs. Agnes Burns
Mrs. Mary Dorsey and her family
Mrs. RoseAnn Williams and her family
Mrs. Nannie Mason and her family
Mrs. Rosey Pendleton and her family
Mr. and Mrs. Francis Jackson and family
Alger's Family
Cousin Florence
Mr. and Mrs. Hawkins and family

Houses on the Left
Mrs. Viola Mason
Mr. and Mrs. Winfield Harris
Mr. and Mrs. Dorothy and David Williams
Mr. and Mrs. Bennie Carter and Ms. Henrietta
Mr. and Mrs. Lowery
Mr. Brown and his family
Mrs. Elizabeth (Sister) and her family
Mr. and Mrs. Longerbeam

27

Marshall Family
Mr. & Mrs. Henry Kent

Shiloh Church
Mr. Robert P. Holmes

Post Office
Locke's Store

Up Millwood Hill
Mr. and Mrs. Junior Banks
Mr. and Mrs. Sanford
Mrs. Doris Green and Family
Ms. Mary Holmes and Family
Mrs. Mamie Jackson and Family
Mr. and Mrs. Marvin Jackson and family
Mr. and Mrs. Eddie Mason and family
Ms. Mary Holmes and family
Mrs. Patsy Turner
Mr. Jimmy Turner
Mr. Eugene Turner
Mr. George Turner
Mrs. Patricia (Turner) Trim
Mr. and Mrs. Francis Pendleton and family
Mr. and Mrs. Spair Pendleton and family

Browntown (Up the hill, just outside of Millwood)
Cousin Laura and Cousin Frank
Mr. and Mrs. William (Futes) Brown
Mr. and Mrs. Cook and family
Rev. Alan Williams and family

Back down Millwood Hill and turn left

Lee Store   Locke store

Millwood Mill
Algers Store
Rev. Charlie and Ms. Bessie Roberts
Mr. and Mrs. Layton
Mr. and Mrs. Francis Pendleton and family
Mr. and Mrs. Carter Jackson and family
Cousin Herman
Guildfield Church
Mr. Penn
Mr. and Mrs. Thornton and family
Ms. Violet Bannister
Mr. and Mrs. Chuck Thornton and family
Ms. Sadie Bannister and family
Ms. Edmonia Banks and family
Mr. and Mrs. Raphael Johnson and family
Mrs. Gladys Stewart and family
Mr. and Mrs. Bismarck Walker Sr.
Ms. Cora Allen and family
Mr. Marshall Mason and family

Millwood

Where my sweet home is just a short distance away,
My heart within my body wants always to stay,
Molded together like generations of clay,
To be formed together representing one day.
Seems like yesterday when we were young,

Waiting and watching for a new day to come.
That day is here far too soon.
Guess what, we just made it to the moon.
All my neighbors have been accounted for.
Maybe now I can close that door
And open an even greater one.
I won the race knowing that I've given full credit to those who came before,
Those who opened up the Door
On an even greater life that shows me more.

CHAPTER 2

WORLD OUTSIDE OF MILLWOOD, VIRGINIA

In 1957, I entered Johnson-Williams High School (JWHS) and began to ride the bus to school. Back then, we did not have kindergarten so you entered at six in the first grade. The school bus picked up all the kids in Millwood at Locke's Store. We were permitted to call them by their nicknames. Phil, short for Philip, and Opie, short for Arthur, were the proprietors of this store, and I must admit they both were good to all the kids in Millwood. They would let us come inside the store in the wintertime to keep warm, in case the bus was running late.

I met a lot of new friends in school, starting my new life at six years old. We didn't have a school in Millwood, so the bus transported us to Berryville, which was about seven miles away. I thought school was a little hard in the beginning because I stuttered and found it hard to get my words out. Unfortunately, the kids didn't understand, and sometimes they laughed at me. I was a meek kind of child, one who took everything to heart, so I got my feelings hurt on a daily basis. I believe there were several other students who had this same problem. Eventually, JWHS hired a speech therapist to come to the school to work with us, and eventually my problem went away.

Needless to say, it took some time to get used to this new environment. Back in the day, I thought my teachers were mean and too strict because I was little and did not understand their methods. As I grew older, I can now appreciate the discipline that was handed down to me as our teachers were trying to prepare us for the future. With time going by so fast, we were in and out in record time. The last time I remember I was seventeen years old and graduating high school; now I am seventy years old. How fast that time went by. Time doesn't wait for anyone. Sometimes it seems to me that a year is not twelve months anymore; it's shrinking little by little. Feels like a couple of weeks have been extracted from the year. Sometimes when you are ready to exit the environment (say, graduate), only then can you appreciate the sacrifices our parents and teachers made for all of us. It certainly takes a village to raise children.

We were taught from the very beginning to have good manners, to respect ourselves and others, and always to be honest. Discipline and hard work went hand in hand and were tools to make our life easier in the long run. I'm not saying that following these examples would lessen any problems in life, but certainly you'd be better prepared to handle problems when they arose.

In school, I always had a problem with understanding the deep meaning of the word *consistency*. My fourth-grade teacher as listed below once left a note on my report card that I needed to learn how to follow through. I actually got upset when I saw that, not realizing that this lady knew me and her other students far better than we knew ourselves. As I have gotten older I look back and can appreciate those words, as they have helped to shape my life.

I am now seventy years young and am just completing this book that I started twenty-five years ago. Wow, it boggles my mind as to how this lady was so intuitive that she could see great potential in all of her students. If I had adhered to these words (*follow through*) early on, there is a great possibility I might had gone a lot further in my quest for living. I just thank God that I am following through on it now. I think she would have been very proud of me for following through, giving homage to her and the other great people that helped to shape our lives. I give honor and homage to this wonderful lady, Mrs. Catherine Marcellus. I believe she graduated and went to college at a very young age because she was so smart.

Johnson-Williams High School gave us the best teachers. The next paragraph will outline my teachers back in the day. I left out a few grades, as I can't remember who the teachers were at that particular time. But whoever they were, I thank God for all of them. It does take a village to raise a child, and God sent us the very best teachers because unbeknownst to us, integration would be starting in just a few short years. Johnson-Williams High School closed its doors in 1966, and we were bused to our new high school in 1967. Sorry, I'm getting a little ahead of myself in that. I want to officially remember those wonderful people that shaped my life.

As I remember back, I now present a picture of some of my teachers:

First Grade – Mrs. Emma Weeks was my first-grade teacher. She was a strict disciplinarian, sort of a no-nonsense type of woman. As I look back, I believe she was the best candidate for this position because she wanted to instill discipline in every one of her students, and she wanted her students to be their very best in their endeavors for life. Mrs. Weeks used a book called *Fun with Dick and Jane* to teach us to read. I believe this book was written by William H. McGuffey in the 1800s. I still remember, that book, Dick, and Jane. I think they had a sister named Sally who had a little dog. We read that book every day.

Mrs. Weeks also taught us this song called "My Hands on My Hips, and What Is This Here?" and by touching our head, we would say *sweat boxer*. We would then point to our knees and say *kneebender*, point to our nose and say *noseblower*, and *breadbasket* would be our stomach. The song ended with us singing, "Nicky, nicky, nicky noo, that's what I learned in school for you." Some of her teaching was through music, and it proved valuable to us because we all remembered well what we had learned through singing. We were taught these values right from the very beginning- First Grade. I will never forget this wonderful lady. Mrs. Weeks also taught us this song, called, "Good Morning to You, we're all in our places with sunshiny faces, and this is the way to start a new day." I am not sure of the author of either of these songs, but whoever it was sure knew kids very well.

Second Grade – Mrs. Luvenia Gillison taught us not only to work hard, but to love others as we love ourselves and always be thankful for the things that God has given us. She also served as our music teacher as she played the piano, and she sang. She was a lady of many beautiful talents and one that was dearly loved by all. I remember her teaching us the Pledge of Allegiance to the flag. This was a part of opening our day so we repeated this every day all the way through the ninth grade. Repetition was the watchword; if you repeated something enough, you definitely were going to remember it. After all, I still remember after sixty-three years.

Third Grade – Mrs. Margaret Carter taught us to have confidence and to believe in ourselves when others might doubt. She was an awesome teacher, a beautiful lady, and always dressed immaculately. She also treated her students with love and respect.

Fourth Grade – Mrs. Catherine Marcellus taught us discipline, building a strong character within ourselves, and showed us how to improve our study habits. She once wrote in my report card that I did not follow through. I used to always look at that as a negative, but as time grew on, she was absolutely right because I always started projects and never completed them. How did she know me that well at the age of nine years that one of my shortcomings was not completing my work? Definitely something that had to be improved upon, so that had to be corrected in my life in order for me to move forward.

34

One day, school had just let out and for some reason, my girlfriend and I noticed that there was something going on out at the back of the school. In the back of the school was a cemetery. We thought we had time before the bus left to see what was going on. We investigated and found out that a funeral was being conducted. We stayed so long that we lost track of time. We then ran to the front of the school to see if the bus was there, and unfortunately, we had missed the bus. We panicked because we both lived in Millwood, and that was about seven miles from school, too far to walk.

We went back inside the school, and to our surprise Mrs. Marcellus was still there; I think she was grading papers. We told her what had happened, and after listening to us, she read us the riot act, telling us to always listen and follow directions and always be where we were supposed to be. She then said that she would take us home. We were never more grateful or thankful to her for looking out for us.

It was only by God's grace that she was still there; everyone else had left the school. It was wintertime, and it got dark early. She didn't tell our parents what we had done; she just dropped each of us at home. I like to believe that our teachers were more than their titles; they were our guardian angels sent to lead and guide us through life. Thank you, Mrs. Marcellus; you were an angel to all of your students.

Seventh Grade – Mr. Robert P. Holmes actually lived in our little town of Millwood. He was an excellent teacher and knew his English like no other. He always expected the best performance of his students and would not let us settle for less. Everyone had great respect for him. He taught us the value of hard work and was truly a disciplinarian. He could conjugate a verb and diagram a sentence better than anyone I knew. He was a true genius at his craft. I also remember Mr. Holmes always listened to Paul Harvey on the radio that he had in the window in his classroom. I still remember Paul Harvey saying, "This is Paul Harvey, good day." I still remember the location of his classroom, on the south side of the building adjacent to the cemetery.

Eighth Grade – Mr. James Ross was our science teacher who was very smart and very intelligent. I remember learning how to dissect frogs in his class. He taught us not to take life so seriously, take time to laugh and always live life to the fullest. He also taught us that in order to succeed in life, sometime you have to take professional risk, otherwise you might not know just how far you can go in this life. He taught us that hard work always pays off in the long run. He truly cared about his students by showing great love and respect to each of us. He always told us that as long as we applied ourselves, we could accomplish anything in life.

Ninth Grade – Mr. David James taught us both world history, geography, and US government. This man was a whiz in government matters. I remember when we had to learn the Preamble to the Constitution; we didn't think we could do it. He then taught us about repetition, repeating over and over until you get it. So true, because we all learned it. I still can recite the Preamble to the Constitution after having learned it more than sixty years ago.

Music Teacher – Ms. Joan Daniels taught us many Christmas songs, and sometimes she taught us songs in different languages. She gave us a love for music and for the piano, which she played so well. I still remember her playing at graduation and working with the choir. I can still hear her playing "Lift Every Voice and Sing." and she would be directing the choir at the same time. She always expected and received excellence from her students. I can still remember hearing her say, "On the count of three, begin singing." She would then count one-two-three, and we would start singing.

She taught us this beautiful song, called "Santa Lucia," which is a traditional Neapolitan song, written by Teodoro Cottrau in 1919. Such beauty in all the music she taught us. She also taught us the school song, which was called, "The Bells of Dear Williams": "I hear they are calling, the young girls, the young boys who come from afar, and so my dear schoolmates, when red leaves are falling, the school bell shall ring out, ring out for you and me." Every time I hear this song, it brings tears of joy to my eyes because I remember those great days at Johnson-Williams High School, my beautiful classmates and our wonderful teachers. Ms. Joan Daniels was a beautiful person who taught us poise and self-confidence. "Always believe in yourself" was one of her mottos.

Math – Mr. Charles Jackson was definitely a genius of his time. He was a master in many things but especially in the areas of algebra and geometry. He was always willing to take that extra time to explain problems to any of his students. I was one of those students who found math to be extremely difficult, so sometimes he had to explain it to me and others four or five times. He was always patient.

In my senior year at CCHS, I almost didn't graduate on time as I was failing algebra, and no matter how hard I worked I just could not grasp it. This man took the time and patience to sit down with me and others to ensure that we would graduate on time. He was patience personified as we definitely presented him with a challenge to understand this Algebra I and Algebra II. He also was our driver's ed instructor—a great man with great principles.

Principal – Mr. Raymond Ratcliff was an awesome man who truly loved and respected each student that attended Johnson-Williams High School. Once when I was in the first grade, he was sitting in for Ms. Weeks, who was out for the day. He was taking up lunch money, and as I recall, lunch cost twenty cents, but I gave him a quarter. He then told me to remind him that he owed me five cents. I was kind of scared to ask for my change; after all, he was the principal, and I didn't feel I could tell him he owed me money. Then I thought, *If I don't get my money back, I won't have money to buy ice cream.*

After all the money was collected from all the students, I was beginning to sweat as he began to walk out the door; I thought he had forgotten. Just before he went out the door, he looked back at me and said, "Don't I owe you some money?" and I said yes. He then told me never to be afraid to speak up, especially when people owe you money. Then he gave me my nickel and proceeded out the door. Thank you, Mr. Ratcliffe, for that vote of confidence.

I will always believe that our teachers at JWHS were hand-picked by God. Not only did they teach school, but they gave us life lessons also.

Kudos to our bus drivers, who had patience in driving us kids to and from school which I am sure sometimes was quite a challenging job. They were Rev. Tommy Jackson, Mr. Carter Jackson, Rev. John Clarke, and Mr. Norman Baylor, and Mr. Grandison was our activity bus driver and substitute bus driver. I still remember that Activity bus; it was maroon and white, our school colors. I am sure there were other bus drivers, and I give all my respect to all of them.

Ladies who worked in the cafeteria—kudos to these beautiful ladies. They were Mrs. Katherine Reynolds, Mrs. Annie Hoesby, Mrs. Amy Johnson, Mrs. Pearl Williams, and Mrs. Effie Clarke. I am sure there were others, but these are the ones I remember during my tenure there. I give all my love and respect to all of them.

These ladies prepared the best lunches in the entire state of Virginia. We were served a three-course meal every day, and these ladies always reminded each one of us that we had to eat up all our food especially our vegetables. Back then I believe lunches cost about twenty cents. It's funny that even though we enjoyed school, the highlight of the day was always lunchtime, socializing with our friends and eating good food. To me their specialty was pigs in a blanket, and if I'm not mistaken, I think on occasion we had hot rolls and fried chicken. We also could buy small cartons of chocolate or white milk for five cents. Of course we always preferred chocolate milk, probably because it was sweet.

Johnson-Williams also offered baseball, basketball, football, and girls' basketball teams. We also had cheerleaders, track teams, glee clubs, and New Farmers of America and New Homemakers of America, along with the safety patrol and library clubs. The teachers were all gracious enough to sponsor each team. This shows the dedication and true spirit of what made this school so great. Needless to say, Johnson-Williams provided its students with discipline, respect, and love, and nowhere in my life have I found teachers of this magnitude.

The year 1966 was when my sister Patricia graduated, and our whole family attended graduation. I remember seeing those graduates march into the auditorium while "Pomp and Circumstance" was playing; so majestic. The young men looked so handsome, and the young ladies looked just beautiful. Mr. Ratcliffe gave his remarks, and each of the teachers spoke very highly of everyone in this class. The choir sang songs, and each one of the students came up to receive their diplomas. The choir sang, "Lift every voice and sing, till earth and heaven ring, ring with the harmony of liberty." It's such a beautiful song, which I believe is now called the Black national anthem.

Johnson-Williams had two floors. The first floor held the elementary classes beginning with first grade and ending with sixth grade. The second floor contained the high school classes and the principal's office. I can recall when the music room was built (somewhere around 1961 or 1962). We were so glad to have a room to sing in.

Since Johnson-Williams was closing down in 1966, this graduation was very sad for me since it would be the very last. Transition to the new school came just a little too fast. By God's grace our teachers had embedded lifetime knowledge in our minds that has most definitely lasted a lifetime. They also reinforced us in respect for ourselves, love for each other, and the belief that we are just as good as the next person, no better, no worse but *equal*.

When we left Johnson-Williams, there were only about fifteen black students in my class. When we entered high school, we were all separated from our friends, and once we got into our classroom, we were definitely in the minority, and we felt very vulnerable because we weren't treated very well. We would pass our friends in the hallway, and we could only wave at them and keep moving. After a while, with what we learned at JWHS and by the grace of God, we began to incorporate ourselves into this school, never really feeling wanted, but this was a means to an end. In my senior class there were 109 students and I ranked number 92. Later in life, it didn't really matter where I ranked. I was just glad to be able to graduate and get out of that high school.

As I have got older, I now believe that where you rank in your class is not going to determine your destiny in life, if you truly believe in yourself. In addition to grades, life experiences also count in your development. However others perceived you to be fifty years ago, you may not be that same person today. My motto is "Grow with what you know." When you're young, people and situations try to bring you to your knees. That is when you check into your brain and fall back on what was taught to you in earlier years. Yes, JWHS covered just about everything. Thank You, Jesus.

Knowledge learned early on means just as much if not more than grades and your position in class. Don't get me wrong: grades are super important in life; they will afford you many opportunities that others might not receive. I have always believed that in addition to your grades (somewhere up the road in your earlier years), you have to have establish a knowledge base. You add to that knowledge base with different events and circumstances that happen to you in your life. You may only be in school for twelve years, but a strong knowledge foundation like the one I gained in Millwood can last throughout a lifetime.

I don't remember too much about this school, other than it presented itself with a definite set of challenges. We had to be our own cheerleaders and support each other as much as we could in order to survive. As I looked back at our years at Johnson-Williams High School, I see that our elementary teachers were preparing us for the real world. They knew that it was not going to be smooth sailing for us and that we would run into a bumpy road every now and then, but soon the road would smooth out, at least for a while. To keep you on your toes, the bumpy road cycle never stops but only slows down enough for you to catch a second wind. The cycle starts over and over again in life; each time you build upon what you learned earlier, keeping the knowledge that you've already learned and adding new insight as you deal with the current bump in the road. Your knowledge base is growing as you speak.

JWHS taught us that some of the best roads traveled were bumpy. I feel that the bumpier the road, the more value-based is the travel. If every road that we traveled were smooth, the journey would not have taught us anything, except that we might think that every road in life is smooth until we run head-on one day into the hard fact that it's not the case. You might have a few smooth roads, but the majority will be bumpy, so I am glad that I learned early on how to maneuver those bumpy roads.

I still have to look back sometimes and remember what I have learned. Bumpy roads challenge your faith, mind, motivation, and spirit. This challenge I believe is necessary to manifest the person you were born to be and to destroy that person that the world wants you to be. I now understand why it is necessary for each of us to reach our plateau. By reaching our plateau, we are then able to contribute not only to our success but to the success of others.

It won't be smooth sailing all the way, but remember that God brought you through the first time, and He will bring you through all the way. Even if each step gets a little harder, persistence always pays off, when we keep one putting foot in front of the other and keep moving forward. Never focus on what others think about you, but put your focus on what you think about yourself: no better, no worse, just equal.

It's been over sixty years since I left JWHS, and I still remember all those wonderful people and their teachings. I can truly say that I am now able to conquer any mountain that presents itself to me. I definitely have not learned it all. What I do know is that when or if I should fall, God's hands are there to pick me up, dust me off, and put me back on the road to recovery. He only lets us stay down for a minute, and then it's back to work again. I have to remember that God is my manager, and I am working for Him. He gives me my assignments, and I have to carry them out.

Learn your lessons, and learn them well, because as time goes on, another layer of complexity will supersede the ones before. If you want to be promoted, you have to study for your test, and the test comes when you are challenged to do something different, something you have never done before. Believe me, it is much easier said than done.

I now realize that God has intervened in my life on just about every occasion and still does to this very day, many, many times. Ever wonder how you came out on top of something with little effort being made on your part. I didn't realize it back then, but high school was my initial look at reality. Today, I can truly thank this school because there, every effort was made to try to push me and others in a downward direction. They didn't realize that we were prepared in advance. As I grew older, I drew strength from this. I learned how to turn negative actions into positive outcomes.

I've learned how to stand up and speak up for those people who can't stand up for themselves. I have learned how to extend myself to helping others, giving to children, animals, and anyone in need. We are all God's children, and we must help each other survive, just as the people of Millwood did when I was a kid. In doing these things we can make a change (big or small) to this world. My high school was my first lesson in *reality*, and I thank you for making me the person I have become, because your realistic if not profound challenge shaped me into the person that I have now become.

JWHS

The place where it all started:

Great teachers that have now departed,

But lessons learned that will follow me forever.

Always and forever a great endeavor,

Life learned lessons that will never depart.

As we get older, they will always remain close to our hearts.

From the classroom to the playground,

JWHS was the very best school in town.

Many dreams given and many students found.

I look back and now realize the value of our teachers,

Who sometimes carried the role of preachers.

Gone are those beautiful ways,

But we will forever cherish those sunny days.

JWHS is forever number one

Because in the end all of its students won.

CHAPTER 3

TRANSITIONING TO WASHINGTON, DC

In 1969, I graduated and left Millwood, primarily to be able to find work to support myself as there were not too many job offers in the country back then. Leaving the security of my home was not something that I initially looked forward to. Country folk looked out for each other; would Washington, DC, do the same?

After graduating high school, I wanted to join the Peace Corps because I always wanted to help people and to travel. I didn't have a firm plan to accomplish this, so needless to say, this didn't work. I remember this man coming to our neighborhood trying to recruit graduates to attend their computer school that was located in Silver Spring, Maryland. In the late sixties there wasn't too much encouragement for us to go to a four-year college. Some of my classmates went to college, but I didn't have the grades needed. I along with a couple of other classmates attended the computer school. I didn't know at the time that this computer training would be the wave of the future.

My first summer in DC, I got a job working at what used to be Doctor's Hospital. I carried trays to patients, scrubbed floors, and did a lot of odd jobs. I really enjoyed working there. Sometimes I would stop by the patients' rooms and say, "Hi, how are you feeling today?" I have always loved people, and it gave me great satisfaction to put a smile on someone's face.

When the fall of 1970 arrived, I started computer school, where I learned how to code utilizing both COBOL and FORTRAN computer languages. We were all young, just eighteen or nineteen years old, and we did not put a lot of emphasis on learning. We were more interested in having fun than actually learning. We did manage to buckle down and graduate the following year.

A couple of months later I applied for a job at Walter Reed Army Medical Center (WRAMC), Washington, DC, as a computer aide. I remember utilizing the SF 71 or 171 to apply for this job. I got a call about a week later to come in for an interview. I was nervous; I had never been on a real interview before. I said a prayer just before I went in. After all, if I made it through this interview, this would be my very first real job.

A couple of days later, I was told I had the job. Halleluiah, halleluiah. My starting salary back then was $4,561 annually, which made for pretty decent money, and I was very thankful. I had just completed my computer school and started my new job; I was on my way. The things you were taught as a child sometimes get lost in the shuffle when you are a young adult. At this age sometimes we think we know it all, to be proven false with the passage of time.

I remember entering the corridors of this beautiful place in December of 1970. I started out at the Armed Forces Institute of Pathology, working in the basement in the computer room.

I loved the place from the very beginning; the majority of the people who worked there were kind and loving people who worked very hard and taught the younger people to do the same. For some reason, we always listened to what they told us, and by listening, we all excelled in our jobs. It does take a village to raise our children, even when they reach the age of maturity.

In the early seventies computers were just beginning to make their way out, and it would be quite some time before we had the internet. I was blessed because I was introduced to computers in the very beginning stages. I was trained on the IBM 360/30, a giant computer that almost took up the entire room. I learned how to use the electronic equipment such as the sorters and the keypunch machines, and I was responsible for keypunching cards and keeping them all in order.

I also had to carry those big trays to the computer room to load them into the computer. Each tray probably contained a thousand cards, which had to be loaded into the hopper. If by chance the programmer had made a mistake, the program had to be cancelled, and the cards had to be reloaded. Each of the keypunch cards were numbered so that they could be kept in order. That was a lot of work. Being brought up in the country we knew what hard work was all about. Hard work and discipline in one area of your life tends to balance just about all areas of your life as they are all intertwined, if you apply that same principle.

Since I was young and had never held a full-time job, God knew that I needed extra help (being at work on time, taking leave, etc.). I actually thought that we would be given a spring break just like in high school; boy, was I naïve. He sent His best, because I worked with two beautiful ladies, both inside and out. I worked with Ms. Lucy and Ms. Libby, two beautiful ladies who helped me find my way through the maze of life. They instilled a lot of wisdom in me, as I was young and thought I knew it all. For some reason I listened to the knowledge and wisdom these wonderful ladies shared with me. They were strict and firm but at the same time loving and caring. They taught me everything that they knew about computers, and they were consistent in their teaching. I feel so blessed that these ladies came into my life at the time when I needed them the most.

They taught me how to run this big IBM 360 computer and introduced me to other young people I could hang out with. I was very fortunate to also be able to work with the computer programmers working upstairs, and they were always willing to teach what they were learning. They were outstanding in teaching me all they knew about programming this computer. They were all very kind and always willing to lend a helping hand. WRAMC was a glorious place for me, full of loving and caring people who looked out for the young folks. Funny how most of the people working there had the very same principles such as hard work and respect for their fellow workers as I learned from living in Millwood.

After a while, I was able to secure an apartment, but it was not close to my job. I had to get up at 4:30 in the morning to catch the 5:00 am bus. Back then it was the DC Transit buses vs. the Metrobus that it is called today. I was a divorced mother at this time and had my daughter in tow. We would catch the bus each morning and then have to transfer at a very dangerous section (some folks thought) of town to catch the bus going uptown. This so-called dangerous section of town (as described by many) turned out to be a godsend to me and my daughter.

The men hanging out on the corner at that time of the morning were men who had fallen on hard times. They actually started watching out for me and my daughter; they treated us with love and respect. I began to feel safe when my bus dropped me off at this transfer point. I was always greeted with a smile and they would lovingly laugh and talk to me and my daughter until the 70 bus came going up Georgia Avenue to take me to work.

I lived far away from WRAMC, so my two computer room ladies, Ms. Lucy and Ms. Libby, got me a ride to work every day so that I would not have to get up so early in the morning to catch the bus. Another one of my angels was Mrs. Edna, a lady who also used to take me to and from work. She was such a kind, beautiful lady who picked me up every day and took me home in the evening. She never charged me anything; she always said that she had to come to work anyway, and she didn't mind.

Most of the people I worked with realized my plight, so one day one of the sergeants told me about an apartment that was right across the street from work. I immediately jumped on it and had an appointment with the manager by noon. I filled out the application and got the apartment the next day.

I kind of missed those guys on the avenue, but I also felt blessed that I was now living right across the street from work. I also found a babysitter who was also in walking distance. This apartment building housed a number of good people, but the Jacob family was one that stood out. When we moved in, Mrs. Eva, who we all called Mother, took us in as a part of her family. She was a beautiful, good, and kind lady. Her children became family to my oldest daughter, who was then a baby. They treated her so nice and kind. Mother worked at a nursing home, and when she went to work, she wore a white uniform that always stood out, starched to the max.

There were other families in the building and we all looked out for one another. When my daughter and I would walk down Georgia Avenue to the babysitters at six a.m., a certain man and woman, whose names I don't recall, would pass me and my daughter every morning and talk to us. They were very loving people, and after a while they would give me some good lessons from the Bible. I found out later that he was a preacher. After a while, I looked forward to seeing them every morning.

There was also a little short lady who was standing at the bus stop every morning, catching the bus to go to work. She also became one of my angels, and she would lovingly hug me and my daughter every morning. It's unbelievable the number of people that God has put in my life, and most of them always came with encouraging words of wisdom. As I grew up in Virginia, God taught me early on to recognize and adhere to words of wisdom, and He always pointed out those good people. I always looked for the good in people.

As my daughter got older, we needed more space, so we were able to find another apartment along Georgia Avenue. This turned out to be a pretty nice place to live, with two bedrooms and still only one block from work. I met with the manager of the building, filled out the application, and went forward to move in. One December night, my daughter and I were watching television. It was cold outside, below 10 degrees. All of a sudden all the lights went out, along with the heat; there was a blackout in DC. I opened up the windows and it was blackness everywhere. I almost started to panic as the apartment turned cold quickly, and we couldn't see anything. I was afraid, but I couldn't panic because I had to ensure that my daughter was okay. I was able to find my flashlight and figured out that my only source of heat was my gas stove so I put water on the top burners and turned my oven on and it got a little warmer, but you can't let your oven stay on when you go to sleep. It was almost midnight and I was tired so I cut the top burners off and the oven off and my daughter and I got some extra blankets and covered up on the sofa. We snuggled up together to keep warm, and eventually, we fell asleep.

As I slept, I had this dream that I was asleep on my sofa, I then woke up and saw what I thought was God and I heard someone say something to the affect that if I reached out and touched the hem of His garment, I would be healed, I wasn't sure at that time what that dream meant, but I did reach out and touch the hem of His garment. I didn't think too much of the dream during the next day, but as I think back, I believe God was sending me a sign, and I am so glad that I listened and heeded His will for me. All of this came to me in a dream. The next morning the lights were back on, and the heat had kicked back on. I remember thanking God, because we were so cold during the night.

I used to sit in my living room after I had gotten off work and watch all the traffic during rush hour. I would say a prayer to God and say, "Thank You, Lord, that I live so close to work and don't have to commute." When it snowed, I would wake up in the morning around six and go out in the snow and just marvel in the beauty of it all. Back then we had six or seven heavy snows during the winter. How I loved the snow and didn't have to share it with anyone because everyone else was in bed. I was always an early bird (this comes from being bought up in the country), especially when it came to the snow.

Along Georgia Avenue, there was an old Safeway, and the manager was a short man with a mustache who was very nice and kind to all of his customers; I think he really liked people. When the new Safeway was built, I walked by there one morning and saw these gigantic lights gleaming from the store, and I thought I was in New York City. How awesome that new store was.

An ice cream parlor used to be on the corner of Georgia Avenue and Van Buren Street, NW. The place had a big polar bear on the outside, and the ice cream was smooth and sweet. The place was always packed, as everyone loved their ice cream. Right next door was a liquor store with a great manager and employees.

I also have fond memories of Ida's department store and Morton's. They were the only department stores in the area, and everyone would be flooding this place on Christmas and Easter. You would run into friends that you hadn't seen in a while; it was always good to catch up. I loved it when my kids were younger as I could buy them nice little dresses, Easter baskets, and Christmas toys. Just before you got to Madison Street on Georgia Avenue, there was a place called Posin's delicatessen; they had the best deli products in DC. When you walked in the store, you could smell the heavenly aroma. There were other businesses up and down Georgia Avenue, but these are the ones that I remember.

We attended Nativity Church, where I fondly remember Father Bouchard, Father Gardner, Father Steve, and Brother Joe and Deacon Harley, and of course Father Q. I love Nativity and still attend that church. I taught Sunday school for over twenty years because I loved working with the kids. I loved taking part in Christmas programs and celebrating Halloween.

In the summertime, we had parades along Georgia Avenue, and everyone would come out and stand on the corner and watch the parades and get back in touch with our neighbors. I also remember the Bivens family, the Murray family, and my special girlfriend Pearl and her family.

Pearl and I started working together at Walter Reed and our children went to a preschool along Georgia Avenue, when they were maybe three or four. How I enjoyed living on Georgia Avenue; that is still home to me, with so many beautiful memories.

Getting back to WRAMC, I also remember Mr. John who was the supervisor in the mail room. I can still see him standing at the Dutch door of his office, smoking his cigar. He was always filled with wisdom and always had a kind word for all of the young people. Part of our day was visiting him and updating him on our lives. He never told us what to do but just provided us with his wisdom, and we made the final decision. We were captivated by his knowledge and caring for all of us. Because I listened to these wonderful people, I excelled in my job at WRAMC. I do think that a lot of what I had learned that had been instilled in my life in the country kicked in at this particular time. I had many other jobs at WRAMC; how I loved that place. There were many others who helped, and I give all due respect and love to everyone.

While working here, I was given the opportunity to make a speech for a celebration during Black History Month. I ask one of the sergeants to coach me, and he and his wife did just that. In rehearsal with him, my knees kept knocking because I was so nervous (this was just in rehearsal), but something inside of me kept telling me to continue on and not give up. This sergeant was very patient and encouraged me to keep on going.

On the day before the presentation, I slipped on ice and hurt my ankle and I said, "Oh, no, I won't be able to wear my heels with my new suit." I probably should have concentrated more on my speech than my physical appearance. I thought I would have to wear low snow boots on stage with my beautiful suit and I was not too happy about that. This was my time to shine, and I wanted it to be at my very best. The day of the program, I took my heels into the auditorium and said a prayer to God to please stop the hurt on my ankle for a short time, so that I would be able to wear my heels with my new suit and look my best.

I sat in the audience and listened to others as they presented. Then just before my name was called, I slipped the heels on. In a matter of minutes I proceeded to the stage, not concentrating on my ankle but on my speech that I had worked so hard on. I stepped up in confidence and delivered the best ever speech, forgetting about the pain that once existed in my ankle. God is good, once again, He bought me through. After my speech was over, the audience gave me a standing round of applause, and I looked up and said, "Thank You, Lord, for this great blessing." I have found out in this life, that you only need to shine once in this lifetime to catch the bug to shine again and again. There's such an overwhelming feeling of pride in yourself, that through God's grace you can accomplish anything.

I also remember walking down the halls of Building 1 (the old hospital) and passing the general in the hallway. He was a tall man with a distinct no-nonsense look on his face. He was commander of WRAMC when I first started working there. There was an auditorium named after him. I was about twenty-five years old, and I used to tell the younger folks, how I remember this man walking down the hallway. They looked at me and asked, "How old are you? You must be really old." I would laugh, realizing that now I'm getting older. But that was okay. I remember one of our commanders who was such a kind and generous man, who knew everyone (military and civilians) by name. He addressed everyone as Mr. or Ms., filling it in with your last name. He was a very professional and caring man.

I worked at many departments while employed there and enjoyed working with all of my co-workers, as they were such great people. I was truly blessed that God put me in the company of so many great people.

I also worked with a gentleman who taught me sign language and another lady who taught me great courage. When I became a computer programmer, I had a supervisor who was a hardworking man who provided us with needed training and respected us to get our jobs done, and we always excelled.

At least four times a year, I have recurring dreams about WRAMC. In my dream, I'm always trying to find a specific floor and due to the changes in the building, I am unable to locate the floor. I try taking the old way (forty years ago), but that doesn't work anymore. In my dream, I say to myself, "Did someone come in here and make changes? I can't find the cafeteria or the different departments. I'm lost."

For some reason, there is always a celebration going on. I also run into people I used to work with, and we get a chance to reminisce. I wake from the dream and find myself perplexed, realizing that these things have now changed. In March 2022, my WRAMC dream came again; this time it came in a different form. There was a celebration going on and the building was all lit up. Everyone was laughing and talking, and for some reason I began to see a little more clearly. I could now find buildings and departments that had been lost to me in my earlier dreams. I now realize where my Washington, DC, nurturing started, and that is why this place and the wonderful people were so special to me. I now had to let the past remain where it was and move on to the future, remembering all that I had gained here in this awesome institution.

Finally, I made it through the door, and there on the other side was a grand celebration in my honor. Change is a constant in life, and we have to put our minds into motion to accept that fact. We can pay an occasional visit, but we can't allow ourselves to stay there too long. Remember the lessons learned, and keep moving forward to the life of our dreams. The training I received at WRAMC was intended for a greater purpose, *a foundation to later lean forward on*. My years at WRAMC were truly fantastic, second only to being bought up in Millwood.

CHAPTER 4

ACHIEVING MY GOALS

Looking back over the years, I have truly been blessed with meeting and embracing such wonderful and beautiful people. The times spent with them have truly provided encouragement to my soul, mind, body, and spirit. The people in my hometown and the people I have met in DC have had a profound effect on my life. This book is written to pay homage to all these beautiful people who contributed to giving me a wonderful and blessed life.

I think God wants us to share the good news of people helping each other in a big or little manner. Big or small, it helps us all. This servanthood to others can make drastic changes in all our lives. Let us just think back and see how far we can go (in our minds) before we stumble across some words of wisdom that were presented to us years ago.

We all have been given advice and words of wisdom when we were younger, that didn't mean much then. Those were what I call wisdom words to be stored in our knowledge bank to be used later in life, when we could relate and fully understand the meaning.

We can learn how to appreciate and love each other, and it doesn't cost anything monetarily, just some time to listen long enough so those wisdom words can take up root in our knowledge bank and plant a lifelong seed. Sometimes I made the mark; other times I didn't, but I would like to say that the majority of those wisdom words took up root in my life. Those that hit my head and bounced off, somewhere along the way, God kept a collection of those and put them back in their proper place at the right time.

I have to admit that I have a problem with disciplining myself, so in order for me to write this book, I had to develop a plan and stick to it the best I knew how. When I found myself getting off track, which was quite often, something would happen to bring me back in line. We can always give advice to others as to what they need to do, but when it comes to putting our lives in order, it's a different story altogether. I had to police myself and develop a plan, a foundation, and a mindset to complete this work.

I kept asking myself why it should take me over twenty years to write a book. As I look back, I realized something about myself. I lacked motivation, discipline, and consistency. I kept telling myself, *I will do it tomorrow*, but tomorrow turned into years and years, and I kept looking back in regret. This time, I was determined to fulfill my mission. When I say that the spirit hit me, this time it hit twice as hard. It struck with a meaning that I just could not ignore. God's way of getting you to fulfill your mission is like no other.

My plan consisted of doing the following every morning. I admit that right away, I got off track and visited non-discipline and non-consistency avenue. After I had been there for a while, I soon realized that I had been there before. At this point, I had lost thirty days and had to find the nearest escape route and get back on course. It's all right to revisit these areas, but just don't stay too long because non-discipline and non-consistency are happy going nowhere.

Plan: Twelve months of training and training continues on

The first month, I started preparing my mind. I had to become disciplined and work with consistency to complete my task at hand. When it came to my children and others, I always followed through, but when it came to completing something for myself, I always fell backward. As I look back, I never really thought too highly of myself, so I never thought I was worthy of anything, so I never followed through. I now believe that one should have respect, love, and discipline for themselves so that they will know that they are worth the time to complete a project designed especially for them.

(1) Start my day around six a.m.
(2) Pray. My prayer also included the Prayer of Daniel:
"Hear, O God, my prayer. Look in favor at my pain.
Hear and act; don't delay, for I bear Your name."
I always added the word *respectfully* at the end.
(3) Drink six eight-ounce bottles of water a day and walk dog.
(4) Listen to the song entitled, "I Made a Vow to the Lord."
The version I enjoyed the best was by the McCrary sisters made many years ago. This song was very appropriate because I made a promise (vow) to God many years ago that when He gave me the title to this book, I would indeed fulfill my mission. I also knew that if I listened to this song every day, it would keep reminding me of the mission that I had to fulfill. When you make a promise to God, you want to see that dream unfold right in front of your eyes, and you have to see it through.
(5) (Also listen to the following videos:

a. From one of my favorite people in the world, Mr. Denzel Washington's motivation video entitled "Put God First." This gave me the spiritual energy that I had to put God first in my life so that the book would (not might) come to fruition. I'm not saying that on occasion (quite a few) I didn't get off track, because I did. That's how I got lost in the beginning because I didn't put God first. I then became a soldier and immediately put myself back in line. When I took my place back in line, I felt a smile come from up above.

b. The second video I watched was entitled "God gives new strength in three ways." I believe the group that made this video was called Crossmap Inspirations. I found myself in this video as He spoke about divine intervention, and I remember how God came to my life and lifted me up from what might have been my deathbed. I was in the hospital in 2017; my appendix ruptured and I had surgery. I was in the ICU as they had me connected to machines and were watching my vitals. All of a sudden I heard, "Code blue!" and wondered what was going on. I was feeling great, or at least I thought. I said a prayer for whoever might be in danger, only to realize that I was the person in danger. I remember everyone running into my room, although I was feeling fine. The doctors looked panicky and kept asking me how I felt. I wasn't really worried because I felt fine. They then hooked me up to additional equipment. I felt that I had to console the doctors. They were there about twenty minutes, I believe, trying to revive me, but I hadn't lost consciousness and was wide awake and coherent. The doctor then took hold of my hand and said, "You are going to be fine." The nurse said that the day before, a patient had died in the ICU. That very well could have been me, but I believe God kept me here for a reason. That is why it is my duty to complete this book while I am still here on this earth. I was out of ICU the next day, was transferred to a regular room and was able to leave the hospital the following day. It was only by God's grace that I am still here today.

In October 2021, my creatinine level was very high, indicating that I might have kidney disease. In December, during the Christmas holiday, I was in dire pain and could barely walk because of the pain in my back. Naturally, all kinds of thoughts came to my mind, Figuratively, I had put myself in the hospital and connected myself to everything associated with this kidney issue. I didn't go to the doctor until January 2022. I went back and had another blood test taken, only to find out that my level had shrunk down to less than half of what it was, taking me out of that category.

Still suffering with the pain in my back, I had a sonogram of my back, still thinking the worse. The sonogram showed that there was a cyst on the left side of my kidney that was not a major issue, and I was told that if I had excruciating pain that I could go to see a specialist. About mid-January by God's grace the pain subsided. God again came to my rescue and saved my life. I had been sitting on this book for so long. Now I had confirmation that God had me here for a reason, and that reason was to ensure that I bring about my gifts. Even today, He still performs miracles for us all. "Only believe, Only believe, all things are possible—only believe."

For the last five years, I had a growth behind my left ear, and I was always afraid to go to the doctor because I was afraid of the diagnosis. Finally, I went to a dermatologist, fearing the worse. My first thought was they have to do a biopsy, and I would have to wait for the results, and my spirit took a plunge. I finally went to the doctor and he examined the growth and said that it was non-malignant but generational, kind of like moles that grow on your body. He said that he could freeze it to minimize it. The growth fell off on its own a couple of days after I left the doctor's office. Thank You, Lord, for grace and mercy.

But they that wait upon the Lord shall renew their strength; they shall mount up with wings as eagles; they shall run, and not be weary; and they shall walk, and not faint. (Isaiah 40:31 KJV)

(6) There was a song that Mr. Glen Campbell sang many years ago entitled, "Try a Little Kindness." This song moved me so much that I included this as part of my ritual to remind myself that the world needs to be kinder to each other. No matter what our circumstances are, there is always someone worse off than we are. Part of our job in this life is to lift up one another. Each one reach one, two, or three, all the way to infinity if need be.

These videos have great significance, but they only serve as a starting point. I had to listen every day, almost all day for a total of twelve months. I had to build a foundation, and I also had to establish my own understanding of exactly what they were talking about. It is true that what works for one might not work for another. The basics are the same, no matter what your beliefs are. I believe that if you listen to these videos long enough, you will establish a relationship with the subject matter being discussed, applying your vision and purpose to the subject content.

Everyone has their own special style; no one's style fits another better than the person it intends to serve. We can use the same principles, but our styles are markedly different. Each of us are uniquely different individuals, and we all bring something different to the table. I used the videos and songs as motivational tools to revive the energy inside of me so that my very best could surface to the top.

Unlike many others, I had to build up my spiritual bank account over a period of time before I could even think of writing this book. Before this book, my spiritual bank account was nearly empty, and most things in my life kind of fluttered without the needed stability to keep anything of value on track for any period of time. Someone once told me that "watching videos can't possibly change your life because you're still going to be that same person." This is true to an extent, that your physical body is still the same, but your soul has been enriched, and that's the difference.

My philosophy is and always will be is that repetition allows us to learn in our own way. Whatever works for you is the path that you must follow. I am now seventy years young, and some of the things I learned in elementary school, I still can repeat today. Repetition provides something like a blueprint of your assigned project, providing you with the opportunity to move forward and begin to challenge yourself to stay on course. The more you repeat, the more information is downloaded into your soul.

I had to establish a strong foundation, one that would stand the test of time and the tribulations of this world. It's funny when you are just about ready to complete a God-sent project, the devil will descend upon you and try his best to turn you around. That is why it is necessary to build up your faith foundation so that you will not get deterred for a time. If by chance you are sidetracked, remember: getting back on track is just a matter of making a right-hand turn in the opposite direction.

Remember, the closer you get to fulfilling your assignment, the tougher worldly issues will come against you, some known and some unknown. Faith will allow you to overcome the ways of the world and keep you focused. Where once you were lost, now you are found. You can now utilize pessimism as a stepping-stone to catapult you to your next step.

When I attended Johnson-Williams High School, one of our teachers—it might even have been our principal, but someone—made the statement, "To thine own self be true," which is a line from Shakespeare's play *Hamlet*. To me that statement means, "Be the person that you were born to be, not the person that the world wants you to be." That statement has stuck with me all of my life. Johnson-Williams was such a godsend to all the students who went there.

I am now able to refocus and put my undivided attention on what really counts in my lifetime. We have a duty to God to do what He asks us to do. If we give Him our undivided attention, we can hear His voice clearly come through. What I discovered really counted was bringing my God-given gift to the world while I was still on this earth. We all have been given a gift specifically to make this world a better place. Some might say, "What can I do? I am only one person." I believe that if you just do your best and treat people with kindness and love, you are on your way. I had to dig deeper into myself because I had this burning itch inside of me that kept telling me that I could do more. That itch, when fulfilled, may make a vital change in the world. We all must satisfy that itch that won't go away.

I have always looked at the world as one giant puzzle that we all fit in. We all have our specific shape (talents and abilities) and size (small, medium, or large) that fits perfectly into our given space in this puzzle. I felt that it was up to me to fulfill my assignment, so that I could fit into my God-given spot on this world puzzle. Some pieces of the puzzle are smaller than others, which only means that no matter the size of your given piece, they all are significant in the sight of God. He knows the capabilities that He has put into us, better than anyone else. Big or small, we all have been called.

I feel that there are so many missing puzzle pieces. Some people have left this world prematurely, who might have gone on to become doctors or scientists; whatever position they might have had, they could have saved the world. Have you ever thought that a person who was killed last night might have been the one who had the assignment of curing cancer? Have you ever thought that young man or woman who was killed last year might have been assigned to cure loneliness or sadness or bring an end to homelessness? Everybody has a God-given assignment that should be fulfilled. I will always search my soul and ignite that burning itch that will not go away until it is fulfilled.

Have you ever said to yourself, *Feels like I have been here before*? Well, you have. You were right on your spot, and you didn't feel comfortable, so you moved. I had to learn to stay long enough to allow myself to settle in and get comfortable. I am beginning now to be able to find my spot in the puzzle, and you know what? That feeling of familiarity, that space pointed out for me, is beginning to settle in, and I am now very comfortable.

My only duty was to complete this book. God would then provide a means to carry it further. It felt as if God gave me tunnel vision temporarily so that the things that used to distract me no longer mattered, as I was on a mission. A mission to complete my mission.

I kept my eyes on the bigger picture. I'm seeing myself on TV discussing my book with another famous author. You have to have something to set your sights on. I am now bringing my book to a wider audience. It's funny what you can accomplish when you're seventy; all those prior worldly experiences add up to a new beginning that you can now put pen and paper to it. You gain that discipline to sit down and complete unfinished work. Time is of the essence. I always reflect on what I learned and then let it take up residence in my soul.

Time seems to get away from you when hours turn into days, days turn into months, and months into years. Most of the time when it hits the year mark, very seldom does that project ever get completed. That is why I am determined this go-around to finish what I started over thirty years ago. Who knows whether I will be here for the next twenty years? God spared my life, so now it was up to me to complete my assignment that was given to me by the Master Himself. In order to accomplish this, I had to *get out of my own way*.

I had an inner fight going on within myself. I fought that battle every day; the stronger I got, the stronger it became. I prayed daily that it would leave me alone, but it never stopped. So I realized then that I had to either fall over and cry or stand up and be counted. I was growing tired of being small and felt an inner urge that something larger than myself resided in my soul. All my life, I had fallen down, and I always wondered what it would be like to stand up and win. Then I thought, winning looked good on everybody else; why not me? I stood up in the name of Jesus and fought for my right to achieve, receive, and believe in my assignment. It was not easy, but nobody said life is easy; you just have to give it your best shot, and God will do the rest.

The annoyance that tried to deter me no longer had a hold on my life. It never subsided; therefore I knew that I was in a fight for my life, and the only way to come through was to defeat this enemy in the name of Jesus and complete my assignment. The harder the mission, the more sacrifice you have to withstand. You use that annoyance to catapult you to your next step. Obstacles can be a blessing in disguise. When I allowed God to change me in this situation, He changed me in the situation. Sometimes you don't know what you're made of until you are put to the test.

You might have prayed for that obstacle to be removed, but I don't think God will ever move what has been put in front of you, to cause you to move to your next step. He just repositions you to a place where you are becoming able to move through obstacles. As long as you are doing God's work, obstacles and annoyances will continue to come to your life and try to stop your progress. That obstacle becomes a stepping-stone for you to accomplish great things in the name of Jesus. Every time you see that obstacle staring at you, say, "Thank You, God, for continuing to allow me to see this obstacle, because it gives me determination and sparks my motivation to complete my assignment." You can literally walk on it, spit on it, or do whatever, because that is what is going to get you to the top.

I want to win now, while I am still alive on this earth and I can witness my efforts to go for a cause greater than me. In order for me to complete my assignment, I first have to educate my spirit. This is necessary to avoid me wanting to drop out again.

This time I had to put on the full armor of God and do my minute, hourly, and daily check-ins throughout the day to ensure that I do not fall back. If I feel myself falling short, I take a double dose of inspiration and get back on the job. I would feel really bad if someone with a similar idea got to the drawing board first, and I had dropped out of the race just as I was about to cross the finish line. I pretend that I am president of my company. In order to run my company, I have to be confident in myself so that when I speak, others will listen, and I will listen to them.

My communication skills (stuttering) that were disruptive in my early life have proven to be a blessing in my later life. A flood was released in my life when I started to believe in myself, and all those bottled-up negative feelings I had about myself were simply released in the sea of forgetfulness, never to return again. I have now learned to speak with dignity and precision and clarity, and that is what I wanted to accomplish all my life. The day has now arrived and I thank God for this great opportunity to uncover this great person that God designed me to be.

My brother Bubby had great communication skills. He had a way of telling stories, explaining situations or even telling jokes so that everybody in the room immediately gave him their undivided attention; he was so informative. I was so proud of him when he spoke, and he had my full attention also, I was so proud of that young man. I used to always wish that I had that ability to tell a story, maybe having to stop in the middle but then pick up right where I left off. I may not be a great orator, but by God's grace I am now able to remember what was told to me in the past coupled with what I have learned in the present and the future to now live my life in a confident and secure manner.

I can no longer hide behind the stigma of stuttering for the rest of my life, I am free in body, mind, and spirit and am proud of the voice that I now hear coming from my mouth. When I released inhibitions, I was amazed at what I uncovered. Go forward, set your plan into motion, and surprise yourself with the hidden jewel that will surface.

I am basically a softhearted person, so when people spoke harshly to me, I went into a corner and was unable to defend myself. That is why I believe that everyone should always speak kindly and lovingly to people, because when you are harsh and rude, you could be destroying one of God's children. Not all hearts are made of stone; some are made of glass and can break easily. Some people recover from a broken heart, others die from a broken heart. Thank you, Mrs. Marcellus (my fourth-grade teacher), for instructing me how to follow through; that is not only a necessary step in school, but it is a lifetime tool that allows you to go from one step to the next. I didn't understand it then, but the meaning now is crystal clear. Mrs. Marcellus, sorry it took me thirty years to complete this, but I got there, and I have you to thank.

I made my prayers a bit bold, primarily because I wanted to somehow make up for lost time. I felt as if this was my last chance at bringing my gifts to the forefront, and I had to make it good. After all, I had asked God for some pretty big things such as (1) homes for the homeless, (2) peace in this world, (3) a Christian husband, (4) good health, (5) a home of my own, (6) finances in order, and (7) a continuing will to give my money, time, prayers, and attention to those who needed them. Not necessarily in this order, but these are the things I have prayed for.

Usually a risk of some kind is associated with whatever we want in this life. I now realize that I had to step outside of the box, and I determined then that change within my soul was going to be a challenging task. We have to want something very badly for us to change a lifelong behavior; faith in God gave me that courage to do so. It didn't happen right away and sometimes I still fall backward to the old ways until I hear the inner voice remind me that I am slipping back.

I can't say that I have conquered it all, because as long as we live, we are in a constant state of learning new things. I just always want to do my best in life. As I am making this change, I keep one of Nelson Mandela's quotes at the forefront of my mind: "There is no passion to be found playing small—in settling for a life that is less than the one you are capable of living." This quote defines what we all are capable of achieving. The cemented ways in my life are slowly melting away, making way for the newly found inner soul that is about to emerge. I have now replaced the words *I can't* with *I can* and *I will*. My spirit now seems to handle the *I can* much better than *I can't*. I believe that once you achieve something big, you will never go back to small. Big can do so much for so many people.

By taking a risk, I will now be able to reach my full potential, which just might lie on the other side of that risk. "One more step and you're there" keeps echoing in my ear. I would hate to die and get to heaven and have God tell me, "One more step and you could have made a difference." I want to make that step while I am here on this earth and hear Him say, "Well done, my faithful servant." If we don't step outside the box, we will spend the rest of our lives wondering what might have been.

Having my arms fully extended and taking that one last giant leap of faith can land me where others have made their mark. Consistency through prayer is what got me here and discipline will keep me here. I feel like you only need to touch goodness once, and then you are hooked for life. I was given a glimpse, and I saw all the beauty and grace that are now within my reach, which gives me motivation and determination to continue on. I so want to see my finished product.

As I get closer to fulfilling my dream, the obstacles are pressed even harder upon me, so just be aware that the God strength that you have acquired along the way is far more powerful than the obstacles coming against you. You're close to the finish line, and there are two runners closing in on you. You keep your discipline and your consistency in check and continue to focus on crossing the finish line. Boom!—you made it ahead of all the obstacles that once stood in your way.

My program also included learning American Sign Language and learning to play the piano. I thank God for the person that I am becoming and am working each day to make that person better.

I also combined my exercise with this song and danced while I was listening to the other videos. On my breaks during the day, I also took care of my fingernails, toenails, and hair. I tried to make every minute of every day count for something, leading to my breakout. I drank plenty of water each day, put flax seed in my food, and had no wine or potatoes and definitely no red meat, just mainly vegetables, fruit, chicken, and fish. In twelve months I went from 189 pounds to 155 pounds, a loss of about forty pounds.

My main problem was I was unorganized and needed a jump start. I didn't want to work too hard; after all, I had just retired. I did a lot of up-front work because of having to build my foundation. As time went on, I really did not have to work too hard. I actually enjoyed sitting down writing, doing my nails, learning sign language, playing the piano, and discovering myself. When I made it a game, by making myself president of my own company (make-believe), it became doable, as I did not want my company to fail. After all, I had spent over sixty years building it up. I learned that things that come easily are usually short-lived and don't have too much long-lasting value. Sometimes we look at things as tedious or hard, thinking they take too long to complete, but as fast as time goes by today, we can accomplish whatever we want in this life in a quarter of that time, if we allow our mind, body, and soul to work in concert with each other and follow God's plan for us.

By God's grace, He taught me the art of self-discipline, by thinking of myself as a world-class woman, one capable of doing awesome things and now following through on all endeavors that I undertake. It's also very important to know that you should try to surround yourself with positive individuals who are in your corner and want you to succeed. Keep those doubters around; they serve their purpose also, and they hold you to your conviction. Allow yourself to see them as such. Thank them for keeping you on your toes.

Once your goals are set, put up an invisible sign that reads, "LIMITED TIME FOR DETERRENTS." Post that sign as a reminder of their purpose for being in your life. Everything that comes through your life has a definite purpose. As the Bible says, there is a time and a season for everything.

For everything there is a season, a time for every activity under heaven. A time to be born and a time to die. A time to plant and a time to harvest. (Ecclesiastes 3:1–2 NLT)

I had applied and was accepted into the University of Kindness and was taking an accelerated course in finding myself. I finally earned my degree (positive, hallelujah, degree) in communication skills. I feel that no matter what you accomplish in life, it should not only benefit you but should also benefit others. The course that was slated to take twenty or more years to complete was now going to be completed in twelve months. I am here to tell you that by God's grace, I have now completed this book, along with combining my other life skills together. My philosophy in this class is Live as if every day might be your last.

Deterrents may come to visit, but their assignment in your life will be short-lived. I now believe that life is to be lived to the fullest. You will run into people who will try to rain on your parade and be discouraging in their remarks to you, but you just kindly say, "Not anymore; I'm on a time frame for Jesus Christ." This time, I have put God first to lead me in this endeavor, and through Christ Jesus, I am thanking Him in advance for the publication of this book. I now believe in myself, even if no one else does.

Straight from birth, God gave me the very best: my grandfather, Albert Burns; my father, Leon Maxwell Burns, Sr.; my mother, Mrs. Agnes Burns; my brother, Leon Maxwell Burns, Jr. (Bubby); and my sisters, Mrs. Deloise Washington and Mrs. Patricia Walker. Thank You, Lord, for all the wonderful people I grew up with in Millwood and those I worked with at Walter Reed Army Medical Center. It has been such a privilege to write this book, and I can now finally give homage and love to all those beautiful people of Millwood and DC who helped me unearth that beautiful person who used to live deep down in my soul. That person has now joined me, and we have become one soul, always putting God in the forefront of my life. God bless you all.

CHAPTER 5

POEMS OF INSPIRATION

Mass Intentions

Oh, verifier of the sea,

Give me confirmation of thee.

Show me where you reside,

So I will have somewhere to hide.

Is it somewhere in the Ebb Tide,

Where so many have cried?

It's funny that we finally meet.

Now, I can finally stand on my own two feet.

I always wondered how I got to be kind,

I looked in my heart, and it was you that I find.

You seem somewhat different than I thought.

Oops, all this time and now you're caught.

This is the place where I shed many a tear.

For some reason, today, I no longer fear.

The walls of this room have now come to light;

It's showing me that I no longer have to fight.

Breathe out, breathe in. You have come this far, and you will win.

Why have I put you to rest year after year?

Must be because I was blinded by fear.

My soul has now come alive, buzzing like bees in a hive

No longer will I allow the universe to misuse my greatest gifts,

And treat them like second-hand stair lifts.

My gifts have now gained momentum and will travel far

By land, by sea, by air, and even by car.

I now uncover the face that had been hidden for years, now take on the Giants,

And have slayed all my fears, entering the Outfield embracing Godly Cheers.

O Infinite Sky

How often do you come by?
Is it once in a lifetime,
Or is your presence always known?
Some of your bravery I would like to own.
Sometimes I walk in fear
That my true existence will appear.
Can you help shed some light
On an already existing flight?
I used to have feelings of delight,
But now I can't seem to stay in the fight.
Please don't leave me on my own.
Your total existence is mine alone.

The Stars Are Shining Bright Tonight

Much to my delight
I now take time to begin my flight.
I feel as light as a kite,
Kind of like a dog that is about to bite.
I am on the trail of a lifetime,
That I will travel only once,
I now see the inner me for the very first time.
I am in awe.
As to what I see, my reflection is staring back at me.
"I've never seen you before," I say.
I just discovered that this new person has come to stay.
For the first time, I see myself full of grace,
A characteristic that can't be traced.
Your mark in life is unique to you;
It comes in only one size that only fits you.
I now sit back and enjoy the journey embracing the
moment that will be the start *anew.*
I don't have a clue as to when I will receive my Breakthrough.
This journey comes now and then and only takes a few.
A journey that I have waited for, for many years,
I can finally embrace it without any fears.
I now realize that I must be my best in everything I do.
I can only be enhanced by suddenly taking a chance.
And I no longer frown,
For it is peace that I have now found.

73

Is That You, My Love?

I see an image of someone above.
Perhaps you've come in the form of a dove.
You resemble someone I believe I recognize,
Not quite sure about those eyes.
Come out and talk to me.
I want to catch you before you again flee.
This has been a lengthy expedition.
I've been waiting so long;
I have to show you that you belong.
You have tried to evade me all these years;
I have repeatedly fought back the tears.
I finally have you in sight,
Leaving you unable to take flight.
You and I have always belonged together,
But separation invited itself in.
And was trying to become a permanent friend.
I have always asked myself if I could ever win.
Why question myself when we are both kin?
We have always belonged to each other.
I then kick separation out and invite togetherness onboard.
I now am receiving tremendous blessings from the Lord.

My Inner Soul – Thru All These Years
I Can't See You and You Can't See Me

Why are you not to be seen?
Are you trying to hide, trying not to confide?
I feel like our souls are not meant to be shared.
All likely they should be compared

Are they the same person wrapped up in one?
If so, our work is just about done.
Sometimes when you get close,
I began to feel the most.

Sometimes I get scared, and other times I am bold.
I guess I am not ready to leave the fold.
At times, you rise up to the front, and then you back down.
Sometimes you cause me to frown;
Other times you make me feel like a queen with a top crown.

I can feel your presence, and I know you are here,
But for some reason I no longer fear.
Can we come together and form a pact
Where each of our duties are left intact?

My vision has improved; you are now coming through.
The blurriness, vagueness, and haziness have all disappeared.
I am now ready to join forces and collide with you in the air,
Bringing together a partnership, forever flaunting our flair.

The Soul and Heart now work together as one.
They both understand that this journey was meant to be won.
Soul and heart, together again as meant from the start,
Each found the other and made a pact; never again will be depart.

I now know that I had always been in the position
To be in control of my situation.

Years

Why do they go so fast?
You know they don't seem to last.
We now look back at our past,
Never forgetting the real reasons for living.
Millwood sure taught us lessons in giving
Onto the stage of life where we now reside.
We are at a place where we can no longer hide.
We've reached the pinnacle where we can now Confide
Into those families, friends, and relatives who no longer reside
That was the Millwood then at its best, definitely at high tide.

Those Wonderful, Beautiful People

Where did they all go?
Seems like they were here only a minute ago.
The number of people living here used to be high;
That is a fact that no one can deny.
When I was young, love lived in this town.
I wonder if that kind of love can still be found.
I'm glad that I was granted the privilege of living here.
When I stop to think of these wonderful, beautiful people who once lived here,
I stop and shed a tear, I miss them so very dear.
God gave each of us a shooting star.
He meant for us to go very far,
To take the lessons learned from the past,
Guiding our lives so that time will last.

78

Guildfield Baptist Church

A place of peace and a place of love,
I believe God senses that, as He looks down from above.
After many years, I still see the beautiful ushers showing people to their pew,
Ladies and gentlemen dressed in their Sunday best, surely outnumbered a few.
This church built a foundation for the Millwood Crew,
choosing all the children to follow through.
We didn't know it then, but we were the chosen few
to ensure that we followed-through.
Where would we be had this community not reared us?
Probably somewhere at the back of the bus.
We continue to say thanks to those who have gone before.
Oh what a blessing to be a part of the core.
Rev. Isham always spoke from the heart,
And when he sang, he delivered a message that will
remain in our heart and never depart.
He imparted to us his love of the Lord, that fact alone will always remain.
I will take to my grave never to be seen again.

Where Has Life Taken You?

Down the path of realizing your dreams,
Driving down the highway flashing your high beams,
Did you make a right or a left turn along the way?
Be careful, you must ensure that you are on the right day.
The difference could be right or wrong.
Was the visit in either direction short or long?
What did you see along the way?
Maybe the difference of night and day.
No matter what direction we take,
Life is never going to be a piece of cake.
Take what you've learned, and do your best.
The world will be first to give you your test.
When you pass, only then can you come up for a rest.
Rest briefly if you must, but not too long;
The game of life goes on and on.

Stop the Violence

We have come a long way to make a new day. No time to play; I am on my way.
Shooting and killing each other were not the ways of our father and mother.
When we were slaves, we held tight to each other,
Willing to sacrifice because all we had was each other.
Perhaps someone looked at us one day and was threatened by our togetherness.
Perhaps someone looked at us one day and said,
"How can I separate this Negro race?"
Stop the violence.
We have come a long way to make a new day, on my way to make a better day.
"In years to come, I want them to develop the tradition
of feeling like a complete waste.
Um! Tell you what I will do, I will pit them against one
another without them being the wiser;
They will transform under me, holding themselves in
bondage like a money-hungry miser."
You know, these acts of violence against one another all started over 200 years ago.
When black folks were considered beneath and below, we
were taught to hate and destroy one another,
So that over the years we would not advance any further.
The same people that spoke this behavior into being now are in their graves,
Perpetuating us into modern-day slaves.
Be aware, the ghosts still roam
In search of an unsuspecting home.
Isn't it strange after all these years we still remain in capture?
Watch out; we might get caught up in the day of the Rapture.

Break the bondage, my brothers and sisters; we have
been captivated for too many years.
Time for action; no more tears.
Stop the violence.
We have come a long way to make a new day, on my way to make a better day.
Strong enough now to put our God given talents into play,
Emerging victorious, declaring victory in Jesus every day.
Institutions of learning will replace jails.
We refuse to continue to chase our tails.
No more jails; they tell false tales of time when we were destined to fail.
I am free, I am free. Just feel those words. I have
learned to fly as free as the birds in the sky.
Be careful, my sisters and brothers; get a clue.
The treatment of the 1800s is trying to make a breakthrough.
Hatred and bitterness is covering this land.
Some are celebrating with the style of big band.
The thief comes not only in the dark of night;
He is now brazen to be seen and heard in the daylight.
Not concerned about the cameras catching their action,
Their minds are fixed on quickly taking a life and gaining traction.
Question is, "Why do you play the part of judge, jury and executioner?
Too many roles for an unforgiving soul."
Throughout time this is how the story has been told.
A lot of us have been left out in the cold.
Reality has returned, masquerading as some unknown.
That same purpose and mindset continue to set the tone.
The 1800s have made a comeback.
How do we halt it to stop their next attack?

Wise up, brothers and sisters; see what they have in store for you.
Let your positive imagination stretch as wide as the ocean tide.
Fill your time with positive behavior, learn new skills you desire,
So that you will not be burned by the fire.
Where there are no jobs, create your own. You set the tone;
You now realize that transition is within your soul
And is a story that must be told.
Go deep in your soul, and discover yourself as a whole.
Question is "How would my Father in heaven want me to handle this?
By using my head instead of lead."
What do you get by taking a life?
You're leaving your brothers and sisters in strife.
We are all brothers and sisters; no matter the color of our skin, we are all kin.
Peace and love go together collectively, where together we all win.
God instituted us all to be our very best.
Let past history propel us to pass that next test.
Earth serves as a training ground for the next world;
Be it heaven or hell, only time will tell.
Be kind, giving, and thoughtful of others,
On occasion having to pick up our brothers,
And the choice won't be hard for God to decide
To whom He will invite into His kingdom to reside.

Extending Beyond the Normal Reach

Are you still here?
Didn't know why I still shed a tear.
That's why I walk in fear.
I just want you to see things clear.
You've stopped and don't know why.
At night I see you cry.
So why haven't you made a turnabout?
Afraid that you might be found out?
Your arm will reach farther than you think.
Quicker than a person can wink,
See how far you are able to go.
God will handle the overflow.
Infinity is out there somewhere,
Calling your name in the midnight air.
Get a move on while someone still cares.
Who are you waiting for?
Someone to come knocking at your door?
Your soul beckons you to get it done.
Turns out it was tons of fun. Besides that, I won.

Life Will Come and Life Will Go

When you die, the whole world will cry,
But I will be hurt the most
Because I was the one standing at the Post,
Waiting patiently every day to be brought to life.
Being neglected brought on so much Strife,
Kind of like a husband divorcing his wife.
I stayed in ready mode each day,
Trying to show you in every way
That I was genuine and was birthed at the heart.
Stayed with you from the very start.
I guess that death will cause us to depart.
That's what happens when you don't put the horse before the cart.
I stayed at the Finish line waiting for you each day,
Unable to cross because of your delay.
I always felt that someday you would have to pay.
The price of neglect is steeper than you think,
And time goes by faster than one can wink.
You're at your grave and have become a slave
To the unknown character that you portrayed.
Remembering that you were mine from the start.
Even at death we will never part.
Cross that finish line today, and put your gift into play,
And believe me that you will be satisfied in every way.

My Dream for Tomorrow

My dream for tomorrow will come true today,
I can feel it in my bones, my dream is here to stay.
I dream of a period that got lost in time,
One with the bells that now start to chime.
I now stride into that dream,
Living has become a part of my daily routine.
I am visible now both sharp and keen,
Standing straight and tall, never again having to lean.
Gone are the yesterdays where I had been corrected,
And onto the tomorrows where I am now selected.
Thank You, God, I have allowed myself to be detected,
Unveiled to the world, appearing now as one of Your Pearls.

A New Day

We have come a long way to make a new day. No time to play; I am on my way.
Shooting and killing each other were not the ways of our father and mother.
When we were slaves, we held tight to each other,
Willing to sacrifice because all we had was each other.
Perhaps someone looked at us one day and was threatened by our togetherness.
Perhaps someone looked at us one day and said, "How can I separate this Negro race?
In years to come, I want them to develop the tradition of feeling like a complete waste.
UM! Tell you what I will do, I will pit them against one
another without them being the wiser,
They will transform under me, holding themselves in
bondage like a money-hungry miser."
You know, these acts of violence against one another all started over 200 years ago
When black folks were considered beneath and below.
We were taught to hate and destroy one another,
So that over the years we would not advance any further.
We have come a long way to make a new day. No time to play; I am on my way.
Stand up! Stand up! And do your part. That is when God will truly bless your heart.
The same people that spoke this behavior into being are now in their graves,
Perpetuating us into modern-day slaves.
Be aware, the ghosts still roam
In search of an unsuspecting home.
Isn't it strange after all these years we still remain in capture?
Watch out; we might get caught up in the day of the Rapture.
Break the bondage, my brothers and sisters; we have
been captivated for too many years.
Time for action; no more tears.

87

Strong enough each day to put our God-given talents into play,
Emerging victorious, declaring victory in Jesus every day.
Institutions of learning will replace jails.
We refuse to continue to chase our tails.
No more jails; they tell false tales of time when we were destined to fail.
I am free, I am free—just feel those words. I have
learned to fly as free as the birds in the sky.
Be careful, my sisters and brothers; get a clue.
The treatment of the 1800s is trying to make a breakthrough.
We have come a long way to make a new day. No time to play; I am on my way.
Stand up! Stand up! And do your part. That is when God will truly bless your heart.

Hatred and bitterness is trying to cover this land.
Some are celebrating with the style of big band.
The thief comes not only in the dark of night,
Now brazen enough to be seen and heard in the daylight.
No concern about the cameras catching their action,
Their minds are fixed on taking a life and gaining traction.
Question is, "Why do you play the part of judge, jury, and executioner?
Too many roles for an unforgiving soul."
Throughout time this is how the story has been told,
A lot of us have been left out in the cold.
Reality has returned, masquerading as some unknown.
That same purpose and mindset continue to set the tone.
The 1800s have made a comeback,
How do we halt it to stop their next attack?
Wise up, brothers and sisters; see what they have in store for you.
Let your positive imagination stretch as wide as the ocean tide.

Fill your time with positive behavior, learn new skills you desire,
So that you will not be burned by the fire
We have come a long way to make a new day. No time to play; I am on my way.
Stand up! Stand up! and do your part. That is when God will truly bless your heart.

Where there are no jobs, create your own. You set the tone.
You now realize that transition is within your soul
And is a story that must be told.
Go deep in your soul and discover yourself as a whole.
Ask yourself, "How would my Father in heaven want me to handle this?"
Answer: "By using my head instead of lead."
What do you get by taking a life?
You're leaving your brothers and sisters in strife.
We are all brothers and sisters; no matter the color of our skin, we are all kin.
Peace and love go together collectively, where together we all win.
God instituted us all to be our very best.
Let past history propel us to pass that next test.
Earth serves as a training ground for the next world;
Be it heaven or hell, only time will tell.
Be kind, giving, and thoughtful of others,
On occasion having to pick up our brothers,
And the choice won't be hard for God to decide
To whom He will invite into His kingdom to reside.

**We have come a long way to make a new day. No time to play; I am on my way.
Stand up! Stand up! and do your part. That is when God will truly bless your heart.**

Letting Your Inside Out

Let your gut freely speak from your soul,
Simple as eating cereal from a bowl.
This way you are no longer blue.
You have freed your soul and found something new.
You now can say what needs to be said.
You find out that you no longer need to be led.

Getting burdens off your chest
Helps to put your soul to rest.
You look at yourself, and now you are your best,
And that you can truly Confess.

Telling others what must be told
Takes a lot of courage, and you have to be bold.
You step out in faith; you are no longer a part of the fold.

Life hasn't always been upright.
Fact is, it's been worth the fight.
You can now float free as a flying kite.

Working from the inside out
Frees your soul of self-doubt.
Feel free throughout your being.
You are at a point to start fleeing.
Free at last, free at last,
You can now live in the present rather than the past.

O Deep Mystic Sea

That lies within me,
Show me what I can truly be.
Secretly traveling in this body for no one else to see.
Wish I had a spotlight to see all that I behold
And to figure out what truly lies within my soul.

Your wisdom lies deep within me.
Today I set you free.
Unlocking a great story to be told,
Something inside tells me, I must be bold.

God knows this door has been locked for too long.
Listen, I am now aware of this beautiful song.
The song says always be great, it's never too late.
I make my way to the open door.
I unburden myself, to the very core.

I will sing the song of a Queen, never again to be lean.
Victory now rings in my heart; words of faith will never depart.
For this journey that I am now on has never been charted,
A new world awakens, and my soul will never be departed.

You have now been revealed, and all your nakedness shows.
I can no longer hide, for I have been exposed,
Revealing my very soul.
What a great story that must be told.

You have now taken up residence in my soul.
I cannot evict you, for you carry the key.
That today, I am set Free.
You are my newly found friend, who will reside with me until the end.

I release you to be free,
To bring about beauty that lies within me,
Transforming my life that otherwise might be
Stuck in the same lifespan for all eternity.

I now move forward to the life that God meant for me.
I picture myself in a forest with nothing but a tree,
Inside that tree, always yearning to be free,
Exhibiting all the qualities that God has meant for me.

For my test of time has now been charted.
I now move ahead in time to catch my boat that has not yet departed
Into a land of endless possibilities, emerging into endless visions.
My eyes are glued to my new mission,
Embracing my dreams with a new definition.
I now perform them with great adulation,
Because I have been lifted, to fulfill my destination.

For it's you that I never want to depart.
You have been with me from the very start.
I now praise you for pushing me ahead.
It's from the bread of life that I now must be fed.

Those who have come before me, so I have been told,
Could not take on the burdens that this life holds.
For some reason or the other, they seem to fold,
Quitting right in the middle before fulfilling their goal,
Only to find out later in life, that minus the strife
Would lead to eternal life.

93

Therefore, my dear brothers and sisters, stand firm. Let nothing move you. Always give yourselves fully to the work of the Lord, because you know that your labor in the Lord is not in vain. (1 Corinthians 15:58 NIV)

Who Will Tell My Story?

When a person who has lost track of reality
Decides in a split second to kill me and countless others,
Sending me to glory before I had a chance to tell my story.

I had an unsettled feeling this morning before I awoke.
It came not as a joke.
I actually heard God when He spoke.
He told me that my life would be given in Sacrifice
To help free the world from its constant strife.

His voice was loving and came with peace.
I immediately felt a sense of release (imagining)
Being absent from the ways of this world's creation,
Being present into an eternity of godly revelation.

Yes, I have been chosen to tell your story,
Even though you have gone to glory.
For those who have killed, I tell you for real:
I was predestined by God to be a doctor,
Sent here to save your father and mother.

Before you pulled that trigger, not once did you think
That we all are connected
To one God whose soul is perfected.
Let's stop and think before we act, for what we do today,
Come tomorrow, will not be okay.

95

Pass the right laws, the ones that will benefit us all,
So that when our time comes, we will not miss our heavenly call.
I believe God is trying to save the world from itself.
We must realize that something exists more dominant than wealth and power.
The hand of God is on us every hour.
He wants us to realize that this world is our temporary home;
Our permanent home lies somewhere unknown.

I have told your story and told it quite well.
At this point I bid you farewell.
Onto the next story yet to be discovered,
Until they all have been uncovered.

This is the beginning and not the end,
Of a world where we can no longer pretend.
We begin to look at the world with a different set of eyes.
By working collectively, we all will Rise.

Printed in the United States
by Baker & Taylor Publisher Services